RIGHT

OF THE BIBLE

IN

OUR PUBLIC SCHOOLS.

BY

GEORGE B. CHEEVER, D.D.

NEW YORK:
ROBERT CARTER & BROTHERS,
No. 285 BROADWAY.

1854.

STEREOTYPED BY
THOMAS B. SMITH,
216 William St., N. Y.

PRINTED BY
E. O. JENKINS,
114 Nassau St.

Preface.

The argument in these pages was constructed with special reference to some labored and plausible endeavors to commend to the Christian community the banishment of the Bible and religious instruction from our Common Schools. These endeavors are made with reference to the demands of a portion of the leaders of a particular sect, and for a temporary purpose; it is the priests of Romanism, and not the common people, nor their children, who would break up our common school system for sectarian purposes, and shut out the light and influence of the Word of God.

It ought never to be forgotten that we are laying the foundations of many generations. Our school-system, and the principles on which we ground it, or by which we alter it, must not be contemplated through the eye-glasses of a present short-sighted sect, or political party, or temporary prejudice, but through the vista of a hundred generations, and a thousand years. To-day indeed we legislate for only twenty-five millions; to-morrow for a hundred millions. Yet the project is up for legislating the Bible and religion out of our schools, and thus providing for the training of the hundreds of millions of the future generations of this country.

The question is not for ourselves, but for our children, and our children's children. The question is not local, but a question for the whole country. It is argued on principles of exclusion on the one side, that apply everywhere; and on principles of religion and of right for the human race, on the other hand, that apply everywhere. If we, in this generation, get the Bible and religion effectually out of our schools, ignoring it, or legalizing its exclusion, and putting the ban of sectarian ignominy upon it, another generation will not be likely to restore it to its rightful place, or to redeem themselves from the fetters of this dreadful mistake. There are those who would establish in our school-system the thunder of the Vatican, with an Index Expurgatorius for our whole school literature; and even good men are fearfully influenced by their sophistry.

"It is a question," said Mr. Webster, "which, in its decision, is to influence the happiness, the temporal and the eternal welfare, of one hundred millions of human beings, alive and to be born, in this land. Its decision will give a hue to the apparent character of our institutions; it will be a comment on their spirit to the whole Christian world." "I insist that there is no charity, and can be no charity, in that system of instruction from which Christianity is excluded." We commend to the earnest consideration of the reader, the powerful argument of Mr. Webster, commencing on page 241 of this volume.

The public mind is beginning to be awakened on this subject. While these sheets are passing through the press, we are glad to notice an able article in the New York Observer, commenting on the recent extraordinary decision of the State Superintendent, founded on the complaint of a Roman Catholic priest, in which the facts of the case have been shown to have been entirely misrepresented. Yet the Superintendent, on an *ex parte* view, has issued a judgment doing great injustice to individuals, and assuming, contrary to the custom and special and common law of our school system, that neither the Bible may be read, nor religious instructions given.

To say that they must not be given, nor prayer be offered, in school hours, is to banish them entirely. The act is despotic, unauthorized, illegal. "Such a position," says the author of the argument in the Observer, "I hold to be not only unsustained by any law, but to be at war with the spirit of our statutes, with the policy of our State, and with the best interests of our country."

From the history, nature, and laws of our Common School System, as developed in this volume, the reader will be able to demonstrate the perfect correctness of this statement. The decision of the State Superintendent, and some of the views elsewhere set forth under like authority, tend, according to the argument of Mr. Webster, to "undermine and oppose the whole Christian religion," and consequently the common law of the land. "In all cases," Mr. Webster says, "there is nothing that we look for with more certainty, than this general principle, THAT CHRISTIANITY IS PART OF THE LAW OF THE LAND."

Contents.

	PAGE
Preface	3
Introduction	9
The Argument against the Scriptures driven to its Absurdities	13
The Christian's Rights of Conscience	33
The Bible not Sectarian	37
Consequences of the Reasoning for the Exclusion of the Bible, on the ground of its being an Oppression to use it	53
The Just Principle of Settlement. Rights of the Majority	58
Supreme Authority and Right of the Bible. Truth more rightful than Error	72
Right of Religious Education by the State. Opinion of Mr. Webster	90
The Bible the Common Inheritance of the World. Opinion of Justice Story	96
Fatal Policy of the Exclusion of Religion. Opinion of Washington, and of the Framers of the Constitution	104
The Essential Requisites in a Common School Education. Case of the Deaf and Dumb	110
Argument from the Nature of an Oath	118
Infidel Aspect and Tendency of the Exclusion of Religion from a Common School Education	124
Argument from the Necessity of Religious Self-government	132

PAGE
Illustrations from Scotland. Argument by Dr. Candlish. Opinion of Bunsen . . . 139
Presentation of the subject by John Foster . . 150
Argument from the Nature of Moral Science . 157
Objection that the Romanists are excluded, Answered 164
Appropriateness and Beauty of the Word of God in our Common Schools 174
Importance of the Bible and of Religious Instruction in the Female Schools. Its interdiction odious 182
Necessity of a Christian Common School Education for a Living and Progressive Civilization . 194
Argument from the History of Common Schools and the School Statutes, in New York . . 199
Report of the Commissioners, and Foundation of the System by the State 205
Beginning of the War against the Scriptures . 215
Establishment of the Free School System. Renewal of the War against the Scriptures . . . 224
Argument of Daniel Webster against the plan of education without the Bible 241
Singular Example of Sectarian Legislation against the Christian Sabbath 257
Common School System of Connecticut . . . 269
Common School System of Massachusetts . . 274
Board of National Popular Education . . . 279
Custom and Opinion of Massachusetts . . . 285
Opinion and Practice in Pennsylvania and New Jersey 293
Conclusion 300

Introduction.

Within a few years, and at the instigation of the sect of Roman Catholics, a powerful effort has been made, and is still making, to divide and break up our system of free common schools. The effort is to be continued and urged with all the energy, authority, and perseverance of the papal power in our country.

Connected with this effort, and fundamental to it, is the attempted exclusion of the Bible and the Christian religion from our whole system of free common school instruction. To advance this effort, arguments have been constructed against the sacred Scriptures as a sectarian book, and much plausible sophistry has been spread through the community, to the effect that justice to the Roman Catholics requires that we should, for their sake, exclude the

Bible at their will, and give to them the power of expurgating the school literature according to their sectarian canons, precisely after the type of that despotic power which is wielded in the Vatican. This would be to place every other sect in the community in subordination to theirs, and to legislate in behalf of *their* conscience, and *against* the conscience of all Christian societies and persons, that reverence the word of God, and claim the right of its presence and influence in the system of common school education.

We propose to show that such a course would be contrary to Divine law, and to all just and equal human law; contrary to the obligations of benevolence; contrary to the rights, and injurious to the welfare of the whole country; contrary to the principles of civil and religious freedom; contrary to long settled Christian precedent and custom, and to the expressed will, wishes, and judgment of the Christian community; contrary to our best local statutes; contrary to the decisions of the wisest statesmen, the most illustrious patriots, and the most learned jurists of our land; and contrary to the history and fundamental principles and provisions of our free school system, as established by the State and supported by the people.

We propose to show, on the other hand, that while it is essential to forbid sectarianism in the public schools, it is *as* essential to bring them under the teachings and power of true religion; that religion should not be driven out under cover of repelling sectarianism; that it is as clearly the right and duty of the State to instruct the children in religious, as it is in secular truth; keeping out sectarianism by keeping in the Bible, and preventing bigotry by making religion free, and bringing all the children under the same celestial light; that the Bible in our schools is the birth-right of all the children, but especially of those who can have no other education but such as the State gives them; that the government is bound, in justice to the overwhelming Christian majority whom it taxes for the support of common schools, to place the Bible and the common truths of Christianity in the course of free common school education; that this is a right of the Christian conscience which cannot justly be refused at the demand of any sect; that it is essential to the security of our laws and institutions, and to the preservation both of civil and religious liberty; that its exclusion would alienate the affections and support of the whole Christian community from the common school system; that education in our country has been grounded in the Bible from the beginning, and that its banishment would be a measure of defiance to the Supreme Being, and of inevitable danger and disaster to the republic.

The Argument against the Scriptures driven to its Absurdities.

THE right to teach the Scriptures, and to have them read in the public schools, is founded on the fact that they are the Word of God for the instruction of mankind. A revelation from Heaven for all mankind is the property of no sect, and cannot be called sectarian; consequently no sect has any right of conscience to object against it. If the introduction of it is contrary to conscience, if the reading of it is an act of intolerance towards those, or the conscience of those, who object against it, then the promulgation of it as an authoritative revelation, is an intrusion upon conscience, and by this argument God himself is represented as doing violence to conscience in enforcing his own Word upon all men, on pain of eternal penalties if they do not receive it.

The Deist and the Atheist have their rights of conscience; and as they both claim conscientiously to deny that there is any such thing as a revelation from God, and one party that there is a God, they may claim also that the use of any book in the common schools that teaches the being of a God, or admits the existence of a revelation from him, does violence to their conscience. The use of Paley's Natural Theology, or of any reading-book that has a single selection from it, or any work that refers to the Word of God as a revelation, or any lesson that inculcates any truth or moral precept on the authority of God's Word, or on the ground of God's perfections, is as truly a violation of conscience, as the use of the Bible.

If it be asserted that the use of the Bible is an infraction of religious liberty, then, on precisely the same grounds, only with greater force and directness, it may be urged that the use of Murray's Sequel, with its admirable extracts from Addison, Johnson, Beattie, Blair, Young, and other writers, is an infraction of religious liberty; for these extracts not only refer to the Bible as the Word of God, and the best of all books, but even assert and enforce its peculiar teachings, with references to it, and quotations from it; so that the asserted rule that a perfect religious liberty requires that an impartial system of public education should be free from any religious bias, is set at naught and contravened in the most pointed manner. In fact, Divine Providence has so wrought in the production of our literature, that it would be a task almost impracticable to construct a single good reading-book from writers of the best style, and in so doing to exclude the element of religion, or a religious bias, as founded on the sanctions of God's Word. Morality itself cannot be taught without Christianity, unless you shut up the manufacturers of your school books to Pagan and Mohammedan literature. But all assertion and teaching of the Word of God, as being the Word of God, all reference to it as a Divine authoritative revelation, all appeal to it, or to God's will, as the foundation or sanction of moral truth, is, by this pretended rule of conscience and of religious liberty, intolerant and wrong, an infringment of the rights of individual consciences.

Suppose I am a conscientious Deist. I desire, as I pay my tax for the support of the public schools, to avail myself of the privilege for which I am taxed, for the education of my children. I present myself with them at the door of a free public school, but am met by a committee with a book in their hands designed to teach the art of reading, and at the same time to form the taste, style, and habit of thought in the pupil, in the best possible manner. That book contains a section on the excellence of the Holy Scriptures. The very title is an offense to my conscience. But when, farther than this, I find the Scriptures referred to as beyond all question the Word of God, a revelation from Heaven for our guidance, with an absolute denial that the soul can be saved without it; and when I find perhaps in some other section, an attractive and beautiful description of the evidences of Christianity, or the grounds on which it is proved conclusively that the Bible is the Word of God; I say to myself, this is an outrage on my rights, a violation of the first principles of religious liberty. I cannot suffer my children to be educated at a school where the instructions I give them at home receive the lie, where they are taught that all that I have taught them is false.

But the committee tell me: sir, this book is one of the best class books in our Public Shcool System, admitted to be so by all, and has been from time immemorial, or ever since its compilation, in constant use without the slightest objection. And unless you will consent to have your children instructed from this book, they cannot enter; for it would be fatal to all order and authority in the school, if the pupils are permitted at every freak of opinion in their parents, to transgress the appointed discipline, or refuse the accustomed lessons.

"Well," I answer, "this is an oppression of my conscience. I would rather have the Word of God itself read, or what you call the Word of God, than these alluring praises of it, and pretended demonstrations of its divine origin." And I have the right of it, if the assumed premises in regard to any "religious bias," or use of the Bible in schools, being an infraction of religious liberty, are admitted as correct. I am, in such a case, deprived of any common benefit of Government, because of my religious faith. I am a poor persecuted Deist, oppressed in my rights and liberties, as a citizen, by the very Government which I support for the protection of both. I am shut out from the public schools, although compelled to pay for the support of them, because the government in them is daring to assume the control of my children's opinions. You are intolerant by system, and you compel me to keep my children at home.

Now, on the assumed necessity of a perfect indifference as to religious truth and error, assuming for belief and unbelief, Theism and Atheism, Deism and Christianity, the same *à priori* claims, the same authority, the same right, or, in other words, assuming that a system of public education, to be impartial, must have no religious bias, and that the Scriptures, as the Word of God, must be excluded, and absolutely ignored, the argument of the Deist is irresistible.

But let us take another case. Suppose I am a Jew, I say to myself—Well, in this happy Republic, and under this unrivalled free-school system, we are at length delivered from the accursed shackles of religious intolerance; we are not compelled to endure the thrusting of that book of fables, the New Testament, in our faces at every turn, and to pay for having our children listen to a lie. Here my children can at length be educated without fear of any religious bias. Under this impression, I take them to the nearest school in the Ward or section of the city I inhabit. But one of the very first reading books put into their hands is a book containing a section abridged from Lord Lyttleton, entitled "The truth of Christianity proved from the conversion of the Apostle Paul." And it is a demonstration that Paul was neither an impostor nor an enthusiast, but a sincere and learned person, miraculously converted from the Jewish faith, to the faith of Christ crucified, and consequently that the Christian religion is a Divine revelation. Furthermore, in other books the truth of that religion is taken for granted, and whole courses of information and of reasoning are built upon it, and the name of its founder, whom the Jews execrate as an impostor, is often referred to, and always with the most reverential and adoring regard. Nay, the New Testament itself, which the Jews teach their children to abhor, is referred to as divine, described in most attractive terms, and beautiful passages are quoted from it. This is an outrage on my conscience, a violation of the first principles of religious liberty. My children are excluded from schools, for the support of which I am taxed, or else they are compelled to listen to instructions and to read lessons which would persuade them that their father is a liar, and the religion of their fathers a deception. My children are excluded from these schools because of my religious scruples, which the government of the schools would thus ignore, contemn, or outrage. And, as a Jew, I am in the right, on the assumption that the use of the Bible, as the Word of God, in our public schools, or the admission of any "religious bias," is a violation of the rights of conscience.

Let us take yet another case. Suppose I am a Mohammedan. I teach my children at home that there is but one God, and that Mohammed is his Prophet. I teach them the Koran as a Divine revelation, and carefully instruct them that all men, except the followers of the Prophet, are infidels, and that none but Mohammedans can possibly be saved. But I pay my tax for the system of free public schools, and I have a right to have my children educated there. But the very day I place them there, they bring me home, as a specimen of the public instruction, a reading lesson, entitled "The spirit and laws of Christianity superior to those of every other religion." The very title is an outrage on my conscience, an intolerant defiance of the claims of the religion of my fathers, the proclamation of falsehood as to all the teachings I have given to my children at home.

But I also find in other lessons and sections, a mode of teaching equally subversive of my liberty and rights. I find the founder of Christianity spoken of as a Divine Person, the Deliverer and Saviour of mankind; and I find the apostolic teachers of that religion favorably compared with Mohammed, nay, and that great prophet himself, entitled the Impostor of Arabia. I find things taught, which, by the laws of the Koran, are blasphemous, and punishable with death. It is a violation of religious equality and liberty for the government to institute such schools. My own children are excluded from the benefits of education by the very religious scruples and convictions which are thus ridiculed and blasphemed. And for this I am compelled to pay the government. I am oppressed in my rights and liberties as a citizen, by the very government which I support for the protection of both. Nay, my very usages and precepts of domestic life, which I teach as sacred to my children, are publicly ridiculed; and under cover of the inoffensive title of "The Love of the World Detected," I find it asserted that Mohammedans themselves, in spite of the interdiction of their prophet, do everywhere, in some part or another of the unclean abomination, eat pork. I find a poem from one of the most esteemed writers of the English language given to my child to read, in which it is affirmed,

> That conscience free from every clog,
> Mohammedans eat up the hog.

This man, again, is right, on the assumption that the recognition and use of God's word is an infraction of the rights of conscience, and that an impartial system of public education must be free from any religious bias. The least allusion to the Saviour of the world as a Saviour, is a "religious bias."

Yet again, we may take the case of a Chinese, a Pagan, a Hindoo. He is conscientiously attached to his own idolatrous worship, and teaches it to his children. Jupiter, Vishnu, Confutzee, or what not, he has the shrine of domestic superstition, and brings up his children in his own faith. But he desires to avail himself for them, of the benefits of the free public schools; for he has his rights as a citizen, and pays the government for protecting them. But the very first thing his children meet with, is perhaps a reading-lesson on common things, declaring "that pure religion is the worship paid to one Supreme Being, the Creator and Ruler of the Universe, but that men through wickedness have become worshippers of false gods, adoring images wrought by their own hands, forsaking the worship of their maker, and deifying even animals and vegetables." This lesson teaches the children of this idolater that his own teachings are all false, and that the only true religion is taught in the life and writings of Christ and his Apostles. Now, this is an incomparably greater violation of the rights of conscience, than if a Romanist had to send his children where the Word of God is recognized and read. It is, by your hypothesis, an oppression of him by the government that taxes him for the support of the schools. You compel him to take away his children, and forego all the benefits of a free public education, or else have them instructed in what he considers falsehood. "His children are excluded from these schools, because of his religious scruples, which the government of the schools would thus ignore, contemn, or outrage." It is, by your own theory, an intolerable oppression.

We will now take but one more case, and it shall be that of the Romanist. We will take it as the others, not now with reference to the Word of God itself in the schools, but to other books, instructions, moral and historical lessons. He pays his tax we will suppose, for the support of a public free school system, and he wishes to avail himself of the benefit. His priest has taught him, and he and his priest have taught his children, that all out of the church of Rome are heretics and infidels, doomed to everlasting perdition; that the so-called Reformation was a great and dreadful schism in the only true church, a piece of wickedness set forward mainly by one of the worst men that ever lived, a licentious, profane, abandoned, and apostate monk, Martin Luther; that the Pope and the papal church are infallible, and that the Pope's followers, and they only, are good Christians. But one of the first books put into the hands of his children in the public schools, contains a speech of the Earl of Chatham, presenting the following passage—"In vain did he defend the liberty, and establish the religion of Britain against the tyranny of Rome, if these worse than Popish cruelties, and inquisitorial practices, are endured among us. To send forth the merciless Indian, thirsting for blood! —against whom?—your Protestant brethren! to lay waste their country, to desolate their dwellings, and extirpate their race and name, by the aid and instrumentality of these ungovernable savages!" Tyranny of Rome, and Popish cruelties! These teachings are against the conscience of a Romanist; it is an oppression by the Government, to compel him to pay for its protection of his rights and religious liberty, and then in the public schools, to have his own religious scruples, and historical learning and belief thus ignored, contemned, or outraged.

But again, he finds the character of Martin Luther drawn by the historian Robertson, and he cannot endure that a picture so contrary to all that he has been taught, and that he wishes his children conscientiously to believe, shall be brought as truth before their minds. It is an infringement of his religious liberty, his rights of conscience, for his children are debarred from a school where Martin Luther is presented as a good man. It is intolerance in the government.

But again, he finds the historical narrative of the execution of Cranmer, Archbishop of Canterbury, extracted from the pages of Hume, and it is against his conscience to permit his children to be taught that Cranmer was a good man, or that the Romish Court was guilty of barbarous persecution in putting a heretic to death. It is an oppression of the government to have this taught in the schools. His religious scruples are in this ignored, contemned, and outraged.

Once more, he finds an extract from the exquisite poetry of Oliver Goldsmith, in which the inhabitants of Italy are described in two of the lines as follows:

> Though grave, yet trifling, zealous, yet untrue,
> And e'en in penance planning sins anew.

This, again, is an intolerable oppression of his conscience. His children have been taught that penance is a rite and duty of the Church, and that those who practice it are good Chris-

rule of equality and impartiality, is the Word of God for each and all.

But the assumption of the argument against a "religious bias" takes the sacrifice of the Word of God on the altar of religious liberty as a necessity at any rate in the free school system; and now, following out these principles logically, consistently, in the formation or expurgation of our whole school literature for the relief of conscience, for the liberty of conscience, where, and at whose instigation, by whose conscience for the rule, for the guide, shall the great work of relief and liberty begin? Shall the conscience of Deist, Mohammedan, Jew, Pagan, or Romanist, be the leader and bear sway? Your argument compels you to the choice of some one, for you reject the rule of the majority, and a mixture of opposing consciences you cannot have, but if conscience be your principle of regulation in the school system, you must take the conscience of some one sect. Whose shall it be? You have already determined the matter. Your whole argument goes for installing Romanism as the supreme deciding authority. You propose the exclusion of the Bible, because the conscience of the Romanist requires it. You are ready to follow the Priest of Romanism at his beck, through the whole region of school literature and usages. You have already begun to do this; and the passages I have pointed out as incurring the excommunicating curse of a Romish conscience, your school commissioners have already obliterated or mutilated, at the priest's bidding; and you have thus made the conscience of one sect the tyrant of all the rest.

And to this day this disgrace stands perpetuated in the school books. The Romish edict has marked its way, as it generally does, so that there is no mistaking it. And it stands a palpable demonstration of the consequences to which this argument against the Bible, at the demand of the conscience of a single sect, must lead. The obliteration and mutilation of the school books is one legitimate result, and some of the noblest bursts of eloquence in the English tongue, and most exquisitely-wrought compositions, historic, poetic, and didactic, must be cut away, and cast out as sectarian, against which the suspicion of sectarianism was never before breathed, the idea never thought of. Compositions of superior acknowledged excellence and immemorial use are to be charged as sectarian, in which no quality or aspect of sectarianism can be detected, because the imprimatur of a particular sect is withheld from them! Because they are *not* sectarian,—because the historian was *not* a Romish historian,—because the poet was *not* a Romish poet, coloring his descriptions with the colors that the church demands; therefore they are to be marked and condemned *as* sectarian, and, on that pretence, excluded! And in the gaps thus made, in the speech of Lord Chatham, for example, the blackening impression is stamped upon the page thus:—

Whole pages were thus defaced at first, because this was a *cheap* mode of accomplishing the Romish expurgation, the remainder of the volumes being still readable. In other pages, couplets of straggling stars filled up the omissions; and, in another edition, the offensive stereotype plate, where it formed a whole page, was destroyed, and pages totally blank were left here and there through the volume. Such is the aspect of a portion of the school literature at this moment.

The Christian's Rights of Conscience.

Thus have you done. But in doing this, you have forgotten or ignored the fact that others, besides the opposers of the Scriptures, have a conscience also. They are, moreover, the overwhelming majority, a point which we shall thoroughly consider. They will tell you that after the Word of God is thus prohibited, and the whole round of literature expurgated of every "religious bias," all the religious element, and even the Protestant historical element eliminated, *they*, in their turn, are conscientiously prohibited, by that very exclusion and elimination, from the benefit of an education by the Government. They pay *their* tax; but the Government oppresses and tramples on their constitutional and conscientious rights, and offers them, instead of a free education, an education fenced round with bars and lances, an education provided with dykes to keep out the influx of Christianity, like the swamps of Holland with their embankments sustained at such an enormous expense, to keep out the sea. It offers them, instead of an education for freemen, an education hoodwinked, fettered, jealous, that like a liveried horse, cannot travel in the public highway without blinders. It offers them, instead of a system open and fearless, producing habits of inquiry and investigation, a coward education, that cannot bear the light,—nay, an education of which one of the fixed and guiding elements is the exclusion of the light; an education that must stifle the voice and muffle the drum of history; an education that cannot endure so much as the mention of the name of Martin Luther, but with priest's curses.

But that is by no means the worst. It is a system of oppression; you fall by it into the very evil for the avoidance of which you have required us, at the conscience of the Romanist, to keep out the Bible. It is an oppression which, favoring every sect in its turn that is opposed to Christianity, sets itself against those only whose conscience binds them *to* Christianity. You have chosen a public school system that legislates in behalf of every congeries of unbelievers, every squad of opposers of the Bible and of religion, under whatever shape, and at their command, arranges the course of instruction, puts the expurgatory brush in turn into the hands of a committee from every one of them, saying in succession, if logically consistent, Now take *your* conscientious turn in blotting out; and resists, disregards, and really outrages the consciences of those only who *love* the Bible, and demand the full historical truth. Have *they* no rights of conscience? Have *they* no claim to a perfect religious freedom? Are all sects in turn to be promoted, and they alone contemned? They do solemnly believe and aver that a system of education which, from being in the outset grounded in the Word of God, fearless, free, unsectarian, yet shining with high religious light, is deliberately altered, is emasculated, is blinded and fettered, to meet the imperious demands of a sect opposed to the Word of God, and becomes jealous against all truth hated of that one sect, being thus sacrificed for a sectarian purpose, is unfit for the children of freemen, unbecoming the republic. They believe that a system of education which thus studiously and guardedly excludes a religious bias, and puts the Bible under a public ban, is in essence and inevitably infidel and deleterious in its tendency; and they cannot conscientiously support it. But you *compel* them to support it; you pay no attention whatever to *their* consciences. Their conscience happening to be in behalf of the Bible, is branded as an intolerant conscience, interfering with the rights of a perfect religious liberty. The conscience of the Romanist, who hates the Bible, and must get it out of the schools, and not only so, but must have the school-books expurgated by the priest, or he will not send his children, you respect. The conscience of the Christian, the Protestant, who sincerely believes that the Bible ought to be recognized, and its teachings admitted, or if they be put under excommunication, he cannot conscientiously send *his* children, you despise; you pay no attention to *his* scruples, you no more regard his deepest and dearest rights of conscience, than if his love of God, and his veneration of God's word, were the most offensive and licentious superstition.

The Bible not Sectarian.

THE question of the Bible in schools is not the question of a distinctively religious instruction as sectarian; it is a confusion of terms and ideas to present it as such. The Bible is the only unsectarian book and system. The Bible is religious instruction, all-pervading, pure, perfect, but not distinctive or sectarian, as opposed to this or that sect; just as the atmosphere is omnipresent, translucent, vital, but not as oxygen or nitrogen. The moment any sect claims that the Bible is sectarian, and therefore would have it excluded, this would be just averring or intimating that they are themselves opposed in it; but no sect will avowedly do that. The Bible, then, is neither Protestant nor Romish. It has never been used as such in our schools; it was never at the outset introduced as such; and it is a slander against those who love it, and a libel on the founders of our school system, to make any such assertion. The Bible is used as God's Word, our guide to everlasting life, and not as a book of Protestantism. If God's Word is against Romanism, so be it; we cannot help that; but that is no good reason why we should hide it from our children, or expunge it from our school literature. If God's Word is against Romanism, it is because it is God's truth; and not because it is Protestant truth.

The Bible is older than Romanism, older than any sect in the world. The Bible is the only Catholicity; the only form in which religion can be taught without a sectarian religious bias; and that is a great and mighty reason why it *should* be taught, or enter in some way as an acknowledged divine element into our public school system. It may be used in a thousand forms; there are already most unexceptionable examples, most admirable compilations of Scripture lessons. It is by no means necessary to use the Bible as a text-book; but selections may be made without offence to any Christian denomination, and still conveying a great amount of instruction from the fountain of light and life. And much might be said as to the preciousness, the invaluable worth of such a model of our native tongue, in its sweetest, simplest, purest Saxon idioms, to be familiar to the youthful mind; a book of style, as well as thought and religion, at that tender age, when every book, habitually read, forms the habit, both of thought and expression, into a reflex image of itself. The dews of elemental purity and power in our language, as well as of heavenly thought and instructions, should thus be permitted to fall daily, gently upon the opening blossoms of intellect.

And here it is proper to notice and expose that artifice of sophistry to exclude the Word of God, by representing our English translation of the Scriptures, as a Protestant or sectarian translation. It is no more a Protestant translation, than the Bible itself, in the original, is a sectarian book. Neither was it ever the particular version, but the Word of God itself, which the translators of our English Scriptures set forth as an antidote to Popery. Unless it be argued and admitted that the Word of God in a faithful translation ceases to be the Word of God, there must be a translation in some shape used. Now, as to the great Conscience argument, of which we shall farther speak, thousands and millions of those who pay taxes for the schools, conscientiously believe that our common English translation of the Scriptures, being neither Protestant, nor sectarian, but the true Word of God, ought to be used; that at any rate it ought to be used till in the providence of God a better translation shall be afforded; that it ought to be used, and *is* used, with no sectarian or Protestant design, but as a thing of equal duty, right, justice, and concernment to all; that if the majority of our citizens employed another translation in their families, which they were willing and desirous to have used in the schools, then *that* translation ought to be used, with the privilege, in the case any particular schools, or classes, or individuals desired it, of using the other translation; but in any and every case, not as a matter of tolerance, but of right. It is the just *right* of those, who pay for the school system, and conscientiously believe that their children ought to listen to the Word of God somewhere, in some way, in the public schools, to have that Word used, to enjoy that privilege; and those who would forbid and prevent this privilege, those who would exclude the Word of God, are the intolerant party; those who, because they themselves dislike it, would make their professed and conscientious dislike the iron and intolerant rule of all the rest.

But the sophistry in regard to a Protestant Bible is so plausible with some, that it requires a further notice. There is no such thing as a Protestant version; there never has been: it is a mere figment, used to cover the attack against the Word of God. There *is* a Romish version, but there is no Protestant version. There is an *English* version for all who read English; the work was begun by Wickliffe, in the Romish Church, before the art of printing; it was renewed and continued by Tyndale, Coverdale, Matthew, and others in the same Romish Church, before the public protestation against the errors of that church. It was printed, published, and circulated by the authority of a Romish king, King Henry the Eighth, with a license, procured by Cranmer and the Vicar-General Crumwell, of the Romish Church, permitting, in Cranmer's words, that it might be "read of every person, without dangers of any act, proclamation, or ordinance heretofore granted to the contrary, until such time that we the Bishops shall set forth a better translation, which I think will not be till a day after doomsday." This very translation, which, in the main, was that of Tyndale, was substantially taken as the basis of the translation issued under King James; it was, in effect, adopted by the forty-seven translators employed by him, so that our present incomparable English translation of the Scriptures cannot be called a Protestant translation, but simply the English translation, and of such perfect freedom from anything sectarian, as between Romanism and other sects, that the learned Dr. Alexander Geddes, an ecclesiastic of the Romish Church himself, called it "of all versions the most excellent, for accuracy, fidelity, and the strictest attention to the letter of the text." The learned Selden called our English translation "the best version in the world."

But it is not a Protestant translation, nor a Protestant Bible, but it is, simply, the people's Bible, the Word of God in English, for those who speak the English tongue. If no Bible but the original Greek and Hebrew were the Word of God, then none but Greeks and Hebrews *have* the Word of God; and if all Bibles but Greek and Hebrew are sectarian Bibles, then the Romish church itself has nothing but a sectarian Bible; her chosen version of the Latin Vulgate is a sectarian version, to say nothing of the Douay Bible. This stigmatizing of our English translation as the Protestant version is a poor trick resorted to in order to banish the Word of God from our schools. It is not a Protestant version, but it is simply a faithful translation of the Word of God in English, for the free use of men, women, and children of all classes and denominations.

If the Romanists choose to use any other English version in the schools, they are at perfect liberty so to do; let them use their Douay version, if they please. Classes might be formed in any or every school with the Douay version, or the common English version, and either be used at pleasure. But for one party to say to the other,—Because *we* do not desire to have the English translation used in the schools, *you* shall not have it, and for this to be enforced as the rule, would be glaring injustice and intolerance.

The Word of God in English is no more the Protestant Bible or the Protestant version than the science of Algebra in English is Protestant Algebra, or of astronomy the Protestant astronomy; no more than the stars in America are Protestant stars, or the sun a Protestant sun. Both the works of God and the Word of God are God's truth. The works of God, this sun, these stars, are seen in England, through an English atmosphere, in America, through an American atmosphere, but they do not on that account, in America or England, cease to be the sun and stars of

God, or become a sun and stars of English or American workmanship. The light is not American light, nor English light, because it pours from the sky, through clouds in the English or American climate, but it is God's light, though it poured through a London fog.

Suppose now, (to take another line of illustrations,) that a poor man comes with his children to a public asylum for something to eat. He is received and placed with his children at a table bountifully spread, and is told to eat abundantly. But suddenly he sees a salt-cellar on the table, and declares that he cannot eat salt, neither he nor his children, nor anything cooked with it, for that he has a scrupulous religious conscientious objection against it. And suppose that, rather than turn the man away hungry, you set a separate table for him, and provide food that has no salt in it. But, meanwhile, the other inmates of the asylum come to their daily nourishment, and sit down and eat at the other table with the salt upon it; and then this man of so great conscience farther declares, that neither he nor his children can partake of food in that house,

unless they exclude salt from the house; that it is an oppression of his conscience to be obliged to eat any thing where others are eating salt, and that if you persist in having salt as one of the regular articles of food in that asylum, you will be guilty of starving him and his children to death, for that he has no means of getting food anywhere else, and his conscience prevents the possibility of his availing himself of the food offered to him there. Would you say that the government are to be bound by the conscience of this family, and that they have no right to authorize the use of salt at all in that asylum? To this extent does the demand of the Romanists against the Scriptures go.

Now, apply this to the case before us. Suppose that a particular family object to their children studying arithmetic out of Colburn's Sequel. It is no matter what the ground of conscience in this case is; it is sufficient that it is conscience that professes to make the objection. The children come to school, and in obedience to their parents' command, refuse to get, along with the other children of the class the lesson set them. They persist in their refusal, till at length they are forbidden the school, unless they will observe its discipline, and use that book. Now, would any man undertake to set up a cry of intolerance and hardship in this case? Suppose there were a score of families and a hundred children united in the same objection. Would the sense of right and justice in the community demand that Colburn's Sequel be excluded from the school, or that otherwise those children were oppressively treated, deprived of the means of education? No, you would say; it is a wilful obstinacy in this case, interfering with and breaking up all possibility of order and discipline in the school, which must be maintained.

Suppose again, that the New Testament is used as a class-book in the schools, and a certain number of children refuse to read that, and persist in the refusal. Is it any less wrong, any less a breach of order and discipline, to refuse to read the lesson in the New Testament, than it would be to refuse to get the lesson in Colburn's Sequel? And if the Superintèndent of the school decides, that unless the children will obey the rules of the school they cannot be received into it, is it any more injustice in this case, than it would be in the case of Colburn's Sequel? The use of the New Testament as a reading book, is no more sectarian than the use of Colburn's Sequel, as a book of the science of arithmetic; indeed, not so much so; for, whereas the New Testament is the pure truth from God, not passed through any human or sectarian system, Colburn's Sequel is God's mathematics, passed through Colburn's particular mind, with his selected formulas, put into his system; as Colburn's arithmetic, it is sectarian arithmetic, and the Romish Index Expurgatorius would have denounced it as such, had he lived in Galileo's time, and been a heretic. But the New Testament is God's Word, and not man's, nor men's, nor the property, nor right of any one sect or denomination. And they who, on the ground of an obligation to their own particular church, should refuse to use the New Testament, and demand of the Legislature not to have it used on this account, would be guilty of the most monstrous intolerance towards all the other churches, or sects, or denominations that claim it, or have been in the habit of using it, and still insist upon that privilege as their right.

The Constitution of the State of Maine declares that, " No subordination nor preference of any one sect or denomination to another, shall ever be established by law." How much more, that no preference of any one sect above *all* the others, shall be permitted, and that there shall be no one denomination to which the arrangements of all the others shall have to submit. Now, the banishing of the New Testament as a class-book, at the demand of a hundred Romish children, the passage of a law requiring the Superintendent of Common Schools in any township or county to do this, would be, in fact, absolutely and unquestionably installing and establishing the one Romish sect in preference and power over all the others. And yet, a public writer has quoted that very provision in the Constitution of Maine, to prove that neither the Legislature nor the School Superintendent have any right to appoint the reading of the New Testament as a class-book, and to require the children who attend school to attend to that lesson! Has quoted that very provision to prove that the Romanists ought to be admitted to make a law for all other sects, preventing them from having the Bible as a class-book!

The argument is, that if the Bible be admitted, the Roman Catholic children are excluded, and inasmuch as the Constitution says that no subordination nor preference of any one sect or denomination to another shall ever be established by law, therefore the Bible must be excluded. But why? Because a particular sect requires it! Then what is that, but just preferring a particular sect to give law to all the others, contrary to the Constitution? And yet this absurd argument will seem plausible with many; and any case where the Bible is used in school, notwithstanding the opposition of a party against it, and where, on right principles, the established custom and law of the school demanding it, the teacher and superintendent cannot do otherwise than retain the Bible, or trample on the rights of all denominations, will be paraded as a case of intolerance and usurpation! Because the Constitution requires that no one sect shall have preference over another, therefore it is unconstitutional to use the Bible! therefore the Bible in the school is a usurpation and oppression! Because the Constitution requires that all denominations shall have equal rights, therefore no denomination shall have a right to the Bible, if any denomination object to it. Is not that an admirable logic of equality and freedom?

The appointment of a reading lesson from the sacred Scriptures, with a rule that the whole class, or the whole school, as the case may be, shall take part in it, is no more an instance of religious compulsion, than the appointment of a reading lesson from the Task, or from the Paradise Lost. If the children were compelled to give their assent to it, or signify their belief of any religious truth in it, then indeed it would be compulsion. But the appointment of a reading lesson from the Bible is no more an oppression upon conscience, than the teaching of the art of reading itself is an oppression upon conscience. Any school exercise is as much an oppression as the reading of the Bible, if any child refuse it, and be compelled to join in it. Yet, to avoid even the appearance of compulsion, it should be entirely at the option of parents to say whether their children shall join in such an exercise. We shall consider this matter again under the example of Scotland.

CONSEQUENCES OF THE REASONING

For the Exclusion of the Bible,

ON THE GROUND OF ITS BEING AN OPPRESSION TO USE IT.

THE reasoning of those who would exclude the Bible, makes the assumption that if only one conscience object to it, its use is wrong. No ultimate rule of conscience is proposed, none admitted; and although the Divine Being has given his Word to dissipate the doubt and darkness of the human conscience unenlightened, and to set it right, yet this reasoning assumes that a conscience without the Bible and against it is of as much validity and authority, as a conscience guided *by* the Bible. A man who rejects the Word of God, has, on this theory, as much right to set up his conscience as the ground in making that rejection a rule for others, as one who *receives* the Word of God, has to propose that Word as the rule. And if the conscience of any person is set in opposition *against* that Word, it is, on the assumptions of this theory, a persecution of such persons to place that Word before them, or to put them in a situation where they cannot avoid beholding its light, or even to offer them a vast benefit, if at the same time the nature of that benefit is such, that their abhorrence of the Word of God causes them to relinquish the boon.

The reasoning on such premises is destructive of the right to spread the Word of God anywhere. Take the Duke of Tuscany's dominions as a pertinent example. The Duke's conscience, under that of the priests who keep his conscience, forbids his permitting any of his subjects to use the Word of God in the vernacular tongue. Now, on the reasoning of those who would exclude the Scriptures from our free public schools, you are intolerant, if you give away a copy of the Bible, or teach it in the Duke's possessions. You go against the rights of conscience, and the rule and reason of a perfect religious liberty, if you, in opposition to the dictates of that conscience, thrust the Word of God before the people. And when the Duke seizes you, and thrusts you into prison, it is not he that is committing a crime against God's Word and your conscience, but it is you that have violated his freedom of conscience, his impartial liberty, which, in and for the education of his people, ought to be left without any "religious bias." It is not he that persecutes you, but you that endeavored to persecute him; and he simply gives you the just punishment of your intolerance and bigotry in thrusting upon his subjects the Word of God. For the Duke of Tuscany's dominions are merely a moderate sized public school, where the experiment of an education free from "religious bias," free from the intrusion of the Word of God, is going quietly on; and you disturb that quiet by your intolerant presentment of God's Word, against those conscientious scruples which the Duke of Tuscany's government is bound to protect. And the district school is but the Duke of Tuscany's dominions in miniature, where you administer an impartial education in the same manner, free from any "religious bias," and with a scrupulous exclusion of the Word of God. You can exclude the Word of God from the common school or from Italy, only on the same ground; a tyrannical pretence of regard to conscience, the pretence that you are bound, from regard to the conscience of those who oppose the Word of God, to exclude it from the presence and hearing of those who love it, desire it, and need it.

On this theory, that is, the theory that a conscience outside the Word of God, and against it, is as authoritative, and as much to be respected as a conscience enlightened by it, and acting under its guidance, if the conscience of the majority bind them to persecute, the minority ought to make no opposition, for such opposition would itself be an intolerant interference with the rights of perfect religious liberty. On this theory, the moment the Romanists should become the majority, and set the engines of inquisitorial cruelty in play in our own country, you have not a word to say; for even if you had the power to stop such persecution, it would be intolerance and bigotry to do it; it would be the oppression of your fellow-citizens, thus to prevent them from exercising and enjoying their conscientious preferences. Nay, if you even have the majority, you have no right so to lord it over the consciences of the minority as to prevent them from persecuting. You have no right to prevent them from burning every Bibl› in the land, or tearing down every Protestant chapel; because, if otherwise, then, by parity of reasoning, if they should have the majority, they would have the right to force your consciences according to theirs. To this absurdity do such reasonings, or rather such assumptions and false premises, lead.

The Just Principle of Settlement.

RIGHTS OF THE MAJORITY.

You object to the settlement of the question as to the Bible by the majority, declaring that "wherever the question of reading the Bible in the Common Schools was settled affirmatively by the bare force of majority, it was settled upon a wrong principle." "Conscience," you say, "knows no majorities." Does it know minorities any more? Does it mend the matter to have the *minority* rule? You are bound to suppose as much conscience on the one side as the other; if a conscience in the minority against the Bible, a conscience also in the majority demanding it. If, then, it is not the bare force of a majority that retains the Bible, it must be the bare force of a minority that excludes it; and which intolerance and injustice is the greatest? By your reasoning, you would give all the positive rights of the majority into the power of a negative in the minority, sacrificing what is dear as a matter of conscience to twenty millions, for the prejudices of two millions. The question is not, as assumed, between a religious education and no education, but between an education in which the conscience of the minority, or that of the majority, shall be respected. If you make the conscience of the minority the rule, you take the monstrous position, in a Christian land, of legislating against the Christian conscience, (the conscience that decides in favor of the Scriptures,) and in behalf of the anti-Christian, the conscience that decides against them. You set up the conscience of Jews, Turks, Infidels, Deists, Atheists, Romanists, Pagans, Idolaters, as superior, as having higher claims, as being, in fact, the standard of religious liberty, against the conscience of those who hold to the Word of God. It is not the professed indifference of liberty, but it is the favoritism of infidelity. You have, in your reasoning, completely ignored the fact that there is a conscience in favor of the Scriptures, as well as against them.

And yet, on the ground of such conscience, by the tenor of your own argument, a system of universal education, supported by the State, cannot exclude the Bible and all religious instruction, except with the free consent of all concerned. It cannot do this, and be a universal and an impartial system. If I am a Christian, and pay my tax for the support of Government, I am entitled equally with my Romish fellow-citizens to all the benefits of Government. To deprive me of one of these benefits, upon the ground of my religion, is an outrage upon my conscience, and upon the principles of religious liberty, without which there cannot be perfect civil liberty. But you do deprive me, when you refuse the Bible and all religious instruction, and thus compel me to educate my children against my conscience, or else exclude them from the schools because of my religious scruples. My scruples in favor of the Bible are at least as sacred, and as worthy to be regarded, as the scruples of any other man against the Bible. The Government cannot any more rightfully deprive me of the benefit of an education, because I happen to have a conscience in favor of the Bible, than it can another man, who has a conscience against the Bible. Admit such an equality, and how is it possible to decide the matter, but by the majority?

If the question be determined by majority, there is a perfect safety; if by conscience, there is not, unless, indeed, you admit the Word of God as of ultimate and supreme authority, and determine conscience by that. If the conscience is to decide, the question instantly comes up,—*What* conscience shall it be, and whose? For there are two parties supposed, and not supposed only, in the argument, but really existing; the one conscientiously opposed, the other conscientiously in favor. Moreover, the one in favor claims a great right and benefit, of essential importance, in the highest degree, and in the most vital direction. The one opposed would exclude and prevent that benefit, for any, and for the whole, on the plea, not that it is injurious to any, but that it is against the sectarian conscience of a part. Which has the highest claim, the positive conscience or the negative? Which shall have his way, the dog in the manger, or the horse that wants to eat? Shall the few that would reject the Bible for the whole, that the few may not have to encounter it, prevail, or the many that would give the Bible to all, because it is a vital benefit for all?

In this case, shall the conscience of the smaller number bind the conscience of the larger? That would be most glaring, absurd, and iniquitous. Shall, then, the claim of the conscience of the larger number be admitted as superior to the claim of the conscience of the smaller? There is no other alternative; and certainly, in all reason, if, as is the essence of this theory, and of this argument against the Bible, you put both consciences on a par, as to right and excellence, the greater amount of conscience *should* weigh against the smaller. If, as you propose, conscience is to be respected, then the greater amount of conscience is to be respected, rather than the smaller, and this, no matter on what side the greater amount is to be found. If it be found on the side of the Bible, it ought to prevail in the right to have the Bible; if it be found against the Bible, it ought to prevail in the right to exclude the Bible. If it be found on the side of Protestantism, (if you will force a sectarian question into the public school system, as you are doing,) it ought to prevail there; if on the side of Romanism, it ought to prevail there. But it is those, and those only, who would exclude the Bible, that have intruded this foreign question of strife and bitterness in regard to Romanism and Protestantism; it was never broached before, never by the friends of the Bible, never by the founders of our school system, with the Bible free for all.

Taking conscience, as your argument assumes, as a faculty or sense of moral judgment, without the Bible, irrespective of a Divine revelation, it is no worse for the majority to determine in a matter of conscience, than in any other matter. In point of fact, a conscience uninstructed by the Word of God *does* know majorities, and is guided and determined by them.

Hence the necessity of that great and impressive command in the Word of God, "Thou shalt not follow a multitude to do evil." So long as no ultimate standard is admitted, (a non-admission which we shall show is the great and fatal πρωτον ποευδος of your argument,) if the conscience of the majority is agreed, it ought to determine. If the conscience of the majority is *not* agreed, it will not be the majority, and will not and cannot determine. But if the majority determine without any conscience at all, or with a mixed conscience, they have a perfect right to do so, a conscientious right, according to the very essence of representative republican society. If it is a matter that does not trouble their conscience, but their will and pleasure are set upon it from considerations of expediency or otherwise, then their *judgment* may be fairly argued as a matter of conscience, and may be fairly proposed as an offset against the alleged conscience of the minority, which, after all, is but a mere blind judgment, without any ultimate certainty. If you respect the conscience of the minority, or of any particular sect, and make *that* the rule for the majority, you may be, and are, in one and the same case, going contrary to the principle both of the majority and of conscience. In respecting conscience in the minority, because it is *conscience*, you outrage it in the majority, whose conscience is on the other side; and in respecting conscience in the minority, because it is the *minority*, you outrage both the civil rights of the majority and conscience at the same time.

Now, as to the case of Romish schools under Romish authority, or of Jewish schools under Jewish authority, you say, Admit that we have a right by majority to teach the Bible in our schools, they would also have the right by majority to teach the Talmud in their schools. The example is badly chosen, because they do not pretend that the Talmud is divinely inspired, as the Word of God, and your proposition admits that it may be. It would better have been stated thus: If we have the right by majority to teach the New Testament in our schools, they would have the same right by majority to teach the Old Testament in theirs. And surely they would. But take it as you state it, and set even the Talmud or the Koran in the balance, and on your own premises as to conscience, they would have that right, as well as on the principle of majority. And it would be the height of absurdity and intolerance to refuse it. You are not obliged to send your children to listen to the Talmud, if you happen to be living under a Jewish government; you have the privilege of giving them whatever instruction you please at home.

But you would *not* send your children to such a school, you say,—could not conscientiously do it—and therefore you assume that it is wrong to have such a school. But this is just setting up your particular conscience as the law for theirs. And by what right could you pretend to do this? They have the right to teach the Talmud, both by majority and by conscience; and are you to play the tyrant, and on the plea that your conscience is outraged by their schools, demand that they themselves shall outrage their own conscience for your sake, and banish the Talmud, which conscience requires them to use, because you aver that it is a pain and oppression to your conscience to hear it? This would be despotism indeed. Are you going to deny to a Jewish government the right to appoint the Talmud in its schools for the thousands who believe in it, because you, as an individual, do not wish your childrer. to hear it? Yes, you say, because you have to pay a tax for the support of the schools. But on your own argument it is better to have schools even with the Talmud, than no schools; so that no injustice is done you in taxing you for that which is as much for your good as for the good of society, even though you profess yourself conscientiously debarred from availing yourself of the benefits for your children.

You say you have the right to demand of the government a school according to your principles, because you pay your tax; be it so; then certainly the majority of tax-payers have the same right to demand a school according to their principles; they have the same right with yourself, on the ground of paying *their* tax, to say what *kind* of schools *they* shall have. Are you ready, by the fact of paying your tax, to claim the right of legislating by your opinion over all the other tax-payers? Have you the right, because you pay your tax, to tell them that they shall *not* have the Talmud, which they conscientiously demand, because you, a tax-payer, cannot conscientiously listen to it? Just so with the Koran and the Mohammedan. On your theory, you would have the right to turn a whole village of Mohammedan children out of school by means of conscience; making the government for your sake exclude the book and the element, without which they cannot conscientiously attend the school and receive its benefit, in order that your children may, with their scrupulous consciences unviolated, avail themselves of its teachings.

It is then, after all, the majority that *must* determine, conscience or no conscience; if you have no ultimate authority, no higher law than the conflicting judgment, taste, preferences, and universally varying conscience of mankind. It is the majority that *must* determine, unless you assume, as in point of fact your theory does, that the conscience of the minority ought in all cases to prevail, or else that the conscience of some particular sect, and that the smallest and most pertinacious, must be the ruling law.

It cannot be made to appear just, that one man's tenderness or scrupulosity of conscience should be turned into the means, or put forward as the reason, for trampling on all the positive rights of another's conscience. One man's preference, in a benefit to which he is entitled, is not to be sacrificed to another man's aversion; much less is the privilege of a whole people in a right and benefit so dear as the freedom of the Word of God, for the education of their children, to be sacrificed, because a particular sect set forth the rule of their Church against it, and threaten to withdraw their children from the schools, if the Word of God be retained in them. Their children need not be obliged to use the Word of God, but may be made an exception; nothing is easier than this. But it is a piece of intolerance and oppression in the extreme, to require that because *they* dislike and reject it, therefore, *we* shall not be permitted to use it and enjoy its light. The thing is so monstrously absurd, that it only needs to be contemplated as it is, stripped of all political distortion and apology, to be seen, known, and felt in its deformity.

We are by no means without examples of just and wise legislation in such a case. Our government has had to deal with tender consciences on more than one occasion; but it has not, as is demanded in the schools, set the example of intolerance towards all others. In the case of the oath, it had to determine in regard to the scruples of the Quakers, who were conscientiously opposed to taking it. If the course had been pursued which is required in and for the schools, at the dictation of the scruples of the Romanists against the Word of God, the formality of the oath would have been expunged from existence; its practice would have been forbidden. But instead of setting up the conscience of the Quakers as the rule for all, they continued the rule, and made them the exception. "There are known denominations of men," says Judge Story, "who are conscientiously scrupulous of taking oaths, among which is that pure and distinguished sect of Christians, commonly called Friends, or Quakers, and therefore, to prevent any unjustifiable exclusion from office, the Constitution has permitted a solemn affirmation to be made, instead of an oath, and as its equivalent." This was wise and just. But suppose, that because the Quakers objected to the oath on the score of conscience, the Constitution had, at their demand, not only blotted it out, but inserted an article or provision to prevent its ever being taken on any occasion, by any person. That would have been very similar to what is now demanded in the proposed exclusion of the Bible from the schools, because a particular denomination are opposed to having it taught or recognized.

SUPREME

Authority and Right of the Bible.

TRUTH MORE RIGHTFUL THAN ERROR.

But we come now to the decisive point, that the Bible is of ultimate and universal authority over all consciences and sects, majorities or minorities. On this ground, and thus only, can we clear away the sophistry that has been accumulated as a *chevaux-de-frise* of prejudice and confusion around the question of a public education, free from "religious bias." The Bible is of no sect, and belongs to none, and may not be ostracised or excommunicated by any, nor rightfully complained of in any presence, nor under any circumstances, as an oppression upon any conscience. The right to spread it, and to teach it, is from God himself to all mankind, and not from man, whether in the social or the savage state, in governments, or sects, or political parties. It is the exclusive property of no church, nor denomination, nor ecclesiastical, nor civil authority.

The argument to which we have referred, against the use of the Bible in the free public schools, on the ground of conscience, confounds the claims of truth and error, and assumes, as a premise, that those who receive the Word of God have no more right to spread that, than those who receive the word of devils have authority to spread that. But in regard to the Bible, as a revelation from heaven, for the guidance and good of all mankind, the duty of making it known is paramount to every other duty; no obligation of conscience towards our fellow-men is clearer than this, nor can any supersede it.

The case stands thus:—You either know this book to be the Word of God, or you do not; if not, then you are engaged in a solemn farce in teaching it anywhere as God's Word. But if you do know it to be God's Word, then you have no right to put a book of fables on an equality with it;—you have no right to permit the plea of another man's conscience as against it, to prevent you from circulating it, wherever you have the proper opportunity and the power. If you know this book to be the Word of God, you cannot, without a glaring inconsistency, which is fatal to the claims of God's Word, admit the conscience of a Mohammedan or a Pagan as of equal authority with the conscience of a man instructed out of God's Word. The conscience which commands the worship of idols is not to be treated with the same respect as the conscience which commands the worship of God. If you say that it is, you are instantly driven to the most dreadful conclusions, fatal to the very existence of Christian society. For the conscience of a worshipper of idols may and does command the worshipper to the commission of unquestioned crime, as infanticide, or the Molochism of the sacrifice of children even in the fire. But, according to the theory on which the exclusion of the Bible from the schools is defended, the theory that the conscience of an unbeliever in God's Word, of a man who rejects it, is as much to be respected as the conscience of a man who receives it, and is guided by it, you have no right to resist or to punish such crime; you have no right even to legislate against it, for that would be a violation of perfect religious equality and liberty. The Government, being in the majority, may see fit to oppress and persecute the idolater who destroys his own children, and to punish him as a murderer; but on this theory they have no right to do it—no more right to legislate for *his* conscience than he has for *their's*. The Government are bound to protect his scrupulous beliefs and conscientious rights as a citizen, a tax-paying citizen, who cannot enjoy perfect civil liberty without perfect religious liberty, nor either, without liberty of conscience.

Suppose the conscience of a person who has married two wives, and becoming a citizen of this nation claims the common benefits of governmental protection and instruction. It is an outrage for the Government in such a case to proclaim his chosen mode of domestic life as sinful, or to promulgate any law by which he would suffer in that state. It would be an outrage in the Government, just because it happens to be in the majority, to punish that man for bigamy; and we prove this, because, "by parity of reasoning," if the bigamists were in the majority, they would have the right to make a law in favor of bigamy. Certainly they would, on the principle of this theory; the same conscientious right, which, when in the minority, it is affirmed should be respected and protected. If so, then, when in the majority, it is to be respected and protected also.

Indeed, the case of the Mormons would have been singularly applicable to show the incongruity of this reasoning. Suppose a handful of the followers of that superstition, with their priest and "Book of the Lord," should settle in the city of New York. They claim the benefits of governmental protection in such wise, that their scruples of conscience shall not be made the instrument of their oppression; they claim the privileges of the Common Schools, for which they assert an equal right with all citizens and tax-payers. But they find in the public school literature some scriptural or historical reading lesson that condemns their whole system of religious and domestic policy, and proves it to be a gross and wicked superstition, contrary to the Divine Law. How can they send their children where their dearest beliefs and conscientious scruples are thus ridiculed and belied? They are oppressively excluded from the public schools; and they have as much right to complain of oppression as the Romanist has, when the Word of God is read in the public schools in the presence of his children.

But we affirm that neither Mormons nor Romanists would have any right to cut and square the public schools according to their church and conscience. We affirm that their superstitions are not to be treated with the same respect as the Word of God, and that they have not the same claim to a conscientious regard. We affirm that there is such a thing as ultimate and absolute truth, and that such truth is in the Word of God, and that no rights, either of majorities or minorities, either of law or conscience, can be pleaded against that, or in exclusion of it, or in ban upon it, to the prejudice of its circulation. The right to teach and circulate it, is the very first right and duty, given and enjoined with it from God to all mankind. No man, nor system, nor any body of men, nor any pretence of conscience, can rightfully interfere against it.

And here we say, and we defy any man on grounds of just reasoning to deny it, that if there be any solemn charge in regard to the children of the commonwealth resting upon the republic, if there be any right vested in the government to meddle in the matter of education at all, it is the right and the duty to provide the children with the Bible, and so to arrange the course of instruction in the common schools, that they shall there come to the knowledge of the Bible. By consent of all who receive the Bible as the Word of God, this is the element of greater power and importance than any other; and it is the paramount duty of the State to secure it for the children. It is the one estate given to the children by the will of their Heavenly Father; it is an estate which every Christian commonwealth is bound to convey to the children, and to apply its interest wholly for their benefit, as guardians in trust. That command by our Saviour is binding no less upon the State than upon the Chistian members of the State, "Suffer the little children to come unto me, and forbid them not!" But you do not suffer them, you do in fact forbid them, if, undertaking their education, taking the whole care of their education into your hands, which, both in theory and practice, you do in the free common school system, you ignore and exclude the Bible and the religious element. You really defraud the children of their estate from Heaven. Oh, but you say, that is none of our concern; they can pick up that estate, or the crumbs of it, anywhere; leave that to the catechisms. A more deliberate fraud and breach of trust was never committed than is involved in this course.

The Bible is unsectarian and pure light. The sectarian schools distribute it as through a prism, but the common school takes it from the sun, admits the sun's light, hangs up the sun itself within the school-house. Now, you might as well shut out the sun-light, and light up your school-houses at noonday with gas because there are prisms, as exclude the Bible because there are various sects. In fact, we have no more right to exclude the Bible than we have to exclude the sun, for they are both God's provision of light for us. We have no more right to exclude the Bible from the schools, and from the use of our children in them, than we have to exclude the common air, and to pass a law that the children, while in the schools, shall breathe nothing but sulphuretted hydrogen, or exhilarating gas.

Indeed, this universality of the sun-light, as opposed to any monopolies, affords us a good illustration. Let us suppose the Manhattan Gas Company to enter a conscientious plea against the sun-light in our school-houses, on the ground that the use of the sunlight prevents the use of their gas, and consequently deprives them of the benefit that might accrue to them and their families from a monopoly of light. Besides, they have among themselves a church canon, interdicting their own families from the use of any light but the company's gas. Under these circumstances, the sun-light becomes Protestant light, for all except those connected with the company, and under its authority, protest against the monopoly of light; *ergo*, the sun-light is Protestant light, and it is against their consciences to endure it, or to permit the use of it; and though they wish to send their children to the public schools, yet they are prevented from that privilege, if the children are compelled to read by sun-light; they cannot conscientiously put their children under any light but that of the company's gas. By that light, they may read and study arithmetic, history, and even Martin Luther's character, and what not, but never by the Protestant sun-light. Whose picture is this, the counterfeit presentment of what faith?

And now suppose you make a compromise, and say to them: well, to make all fair, you shall have the privilege of introducing the gas-light for *your* children, but at the same time the sun-light shall come in also, so that all may be satisfied. Ah, but that will not answer; the sun-light must not be let in at all, for wherever it is, it absolutely puts theirs out.

'Tis of no use whatever, they say, to attempt a competition; it is a gone case with us, if the sun-light is let in at all. Our gas, in competition with the sun? Why, the children would read on, and read on, and not even know that our gas was lighted.

Well! so it is, in very truth, and we cannot help it, that the Bible really does give so clear and beautiful, so pure and powerful a light, that all other lights beside it are but winking tapers, and you can scarcely even see that they are lighted. In the language of Cowper's exquisitely beautiful hymn,

> A Glory gilds the sacred page,
> Majestic like the sun;
> It give a light to every age,
> It gives, but borrows none.

Nay, according to God's own declaration concerning it, you determine by it infallibly what *is* light, and whether other things proposed as light are not darkness. "In thy light, shall we see light." We shall see and know what the true light is, and not be imposed upon.

This common, all surrounding, vital air is not more my right to breathe, and yours, and all men's, than this air of Divine Truth, which is to the life and healthful movement of the soul, what the air is to the lungs, to the blood, and to the life of the body. You have no more right to interdict this atmosphere of Divine Truth, than you have to interdict the pure air of Heaven from our school houses. Nor is an imperfect or vicious ventilation so bad for the body, as the interdiction of the fresh air of truth is pernicious to the soul. Stifle out of it all religious truth, and it will die, not of suffocation merely, but of poison with malignant error. Shall this be the treatment of the millions of youthful immortal creatures crowded in our common schools as in a dungeon? No, no, no! but let all the windows, as in a clear summer's day in the country, be thrown wide open, and let the sweet breath from every wind of Heaven flow through, joyful, balmy, exhilarating. Let the gladsome troops of children breathe freely, and not begin their first rudiments of knowledge by trying how far they can be stifled, and still live,

This common, all-shining sun is no more my right to see by, to have its cheerful beams pour warm and bright upon me, wherever in the world I am, than this Sun of God's Truth in his Word is my right of conscience and of heavenly life. This Sun of truth is as truly the possession of all mankind, and the gift of God for the race, as the sun in the heavens, and as necessary for the light and life of the soul as the sun for the light and life of the body. Who dare interdict the sun from shining, or men from looking at his light? What vain Canute would lift his puny sceptre to that orb, and say, as Lucifer from Hell, I speak to thee, O Sun, only to tell thee how I hate thy beams! And is it less a blasphemous defiance of God to interdict his Word, and to say to the creatures for whom it was given, ye shall not enjoy it? This Word of God is as necessary for our perception of moral truth, as the sun is necessary for our perception of colors in nature; it is as essential for the growth of true moral principle, and the right development of our immortal being, as the light of the sun is necessary for the growth of plants, fruits, and flowers. When the sun goes down in either case, it is night, and all the beasts of the earth come forth from their hiding places. What infinite madness to introduce into the constitution and custom or common law of our school system as one of its guiding central principles, the exclusion of Divine light! If the country were bent on self-destruction, it could hardly discover a subtler and surer mode of suicide. Volcanoes and earthquakes are said to have been heralded by the drying up of wells; and so, there is no convulsion or evil which may not be apprehended, if from the fountains of our common education, the elements of Divine truth are drawn away; it would be the most certain prophecy of evil.

Now, if we take simply the ground of the great command of God and our conscience, Thou shalt love thy neighbor as thyself, on that ground, whatever we find to be essential to our own life and welfare as human beings, we are bound to give to others, if we have it in our power. If the Word of God is dear to us, and we know it to be essential to salvation, we are bound to give it to others; if necessary to me as an individual, I have no more right to it myself, than I have to communicate it to others; both the right and the duty are incontrovertible. Neither man, nor men, nor governments, nor hierarchies, have any more right to say to me, You shall not spread the Word of God, than they would have to say to me, You shall not give a morsel of bread to the wretch whom you see dying of hunger. It is both my right and my duty from God.

But not only is it mine, but of humanity, of nations, of all mankind. And whatever country, or people, set up enactments against this right and duty, they are, so far, outlawed of God and of conscience, and such enactments are not to be regarded in the least. Any nation, and any church, that makes the use, enjoyment, and distribution of the Word of God a crime, is out of the pale of international law and of human right, and against it, and ought to be treated accordingly. We like the language of Captain Packenham, of the English Navy, that energetic and fearless soldier of Christ, who undertook to distribute Bibles and religious truth in Italy. "It is time," says he, speaking of the case of Miss Cunninghame's imprisonment and release by the Duke of Tuscany, "that our *rights* should be acknowledged and respected. Let it be known that we are not to receive as a grace, that which justice demands as a right. It is time that diplomacy cease to sue *in forma pauperis*, and that individual favoritism, however arrived at, give place to a well understood, authoritative demand, so well expressed in our royal motto, God and our right. It is time to say to this manufactory of delinquencies and crimes, this modern inquisition, Stop! Whatever be not really a crime, your pigmy, paltry, Papal legislation shall not make one; and if you dare to punish a free-born subject of England, by the application of your penal proclamations or processes, you shall repent it quickly."

Clearly, this is the only right and safe position. Christianity, based upon the Word of God, is the gift of God to all, and as it respects Europe, it is the profession of all nations. Shall any then dare, or shall they be permitted, to make it a crime to circulate the Word of God? This is the common right of all to whom that Word comes, and the prohibition of it by the Roman Catholic Church, in Tuscany, for example—Church and State being one—is well set forth as being a complete self-condemnation, a demonstration of not being within the pale of true Christianity. It is a glaring syllogism, fiery red with shame. To circulate any book which is contrary to the Roman Catholic religion is made a legal crime. But to circulate the Word of God is prohibited as such a crime, and an English lady was thrown into prison for doing it. Consequently, the Word of God is clearly proclaimed as being contrary to the Roman Catholic religion. This is the inevitable logic of the Government of the Duke of Tuscany.

But with this particular conclusion of the Duke's logic, we need not now concern ourselves; the point in view is the iniquity of its application—the injustice of any law or laws against the Word of God, forbidding its use and circulation. Even in the bosom of the Romish Church, the very first translators of the Scriptures into English felt this. When the youthful Tyndale began first to have his eyes opened to the truth, and to form the purpose, by God's blessing, in after years, to give the Word of God in English to the people, he saw that it was the right of all mankind, for that it was the gift of God to all. The indignant speeches that fell from him, even then, exposed him to danger. In controversy with an ignorant Romish ecclesiastic, he one day said, "If God spare my life, ere many years I will cause a boy that driveth the plow, to know more of the Scripture than you do." But how were the plowboys to know it, if it should be excluded by law from the system of education, on pretence of liberality of conscience? In vain would the noble Tyndale's prophecy have been fulfilled, and his mission-task performed and sealed with martyrdom, for the plow-boys of his country, if the translation of the Scriptures was to be excluded from the schools, as a sectarian book, or forbidden, on the plea of its going against the Romish conscience.

Right of Religious Education by the State.

OPINION OF MR. WEBSTER.

"THE Government," says Hugh Miller, "that should imprison with punishment or death the man whose only crime was, that he had given a morsel of bread to a dying beggar, or rescued some unhappy human being who was in danger of perishing in the pit into which he had fallen, would be held to have violated the *rights of man*, if the person so punished was a subject of its own, and the *rights of nations*, if he was the subject of another State. But does not that Government as really violate the rights of man, and the laws of Christian nations, which says, you shall not give a copy of the Bible to a human being, however desirous he may be to know the will of his Maker, and however much he may feel that his eternal welfare depends on knowing that will? The Government that should act thus would so violate the first right of conscience and the first duties of man, and so uproot the foundations of society, as to place itself beyond the pale of civilized nations; it ought to be declared an outlaw,—a nation at war with the eternal principles of duty and right, and entitled to exact no regard or obedience to its laws."

Now, let us just apply these principles to the right and duty of providing the children in our common schools with the Word of God, and with the religious instruction they may receive from it, and thus judge and determine the iniquity of any statute for the exclusion of the Bible. Such a statute, whether in legislative act and form, or merely the force of prejudice and custom wrought into a common law, would be glaringly inconsistent with the duty of the State, and with our rights as individuals. And what an incongruity would it present, while the common law of the State is based upon Christianity, and in favor of it, to have the common law of the schools excluding it, and so in reality against it. The argument by which the opponents of the Bible, in schools, would support their views, goes the whole length of denying to the State the right of religious instruction, because it is asserted to be an oppression of the conscience. And the demand is made of a wholesale exclusion of all religious bias, because otherwise the State cannot be impartial to her children. But let us hear the voice of some of our greatest and wisest statesmen on this matter.

In speaking on the subject of taxation for public education, Mr. Webster once said: "We seek to prevent, in some measure, the extension of the penal code, by inspiring a salutary and conservative principle of virtue and of knowledge in an early age. By general instruction, we seek as far as possible to purify the whole moral atmosphere; to keep good sentiment uppermost, and to turn the strong current of feeling and opinion, as well as the censures of the law and the denunciations of religion, against immorality and crime. We hope for a security beyond the law, and above the law, in the prevalence of enlightened and well-principled moral sentiment. We hope to continue and to prolong the time, when in the villages and farm-houses of New England there may be undisturbed sleep within unbarred doors."

Mr. Webster was a man that weighed his words. And now in perusing the succeeding paragraph, let it be remembered that this speech was on an occasion that demanded the greatest solidity and accuracy in the formation and expression of his views, being no less important than the revision of the Constitution of the State of Massachusetts. His opinions were, therefore, deliberate and well considered, and they are decisive as to the power and duty of the State to provide a religious education for her children, if an education at all.

"I rejoice that every man in this community can call all property his own, so far as he has occasion for it to furnish for himself and his children the blessings of religious instruction, and the elements of knowledge. This celestial and this earthly light he is entitled to by the fundamental laws. It is every poor man's undoubted birthright; it is the great blessing which this Constitution has secured to him; it is his solace in life, and it may well be his consolation in death, that his country stands pledged by the faith which it has plighted to all its citizens, to protect his children from ignorance, barbarism, and vice."

These are noble words, and the speech bears the stamp of Webster's magnificent mind. The children of the State are entitled by the fundamental law to a celestial as well as earthly light, and to the blessings of religious instruction, as well as the elements of other knowledge. The assertion would seem a truism; and yet we are aware of the plausible sophistry with which a decision right the reverse is maintained in some quarters, and proposed as a fundamental school law; the decision to exclude all celestial light as sectarian, and all religious instruction as an oppression of the conscience.

But if the State undertake to educate the children at all, is it not under obligation to give them as good an education as they can get elsewhere? If the State tax its citizens for the expenses of such an education, does it not stand pledged to teach the children of the citizens all that is essential to their welfare? Is it a fulfilment of that pledge to say that they may get religious instruction elsewhere, but that the State shall not provide that vital element, for fear of sectarianism? *May* get it elsewhere! And who stands responsible for the consequences, if they should *not?*

The Bible the Common Inheritance of the World.

OPINION OF JUSTICE STORY.

In dwelling on the liberty of speech, and the importance of securing it, that great writer on the Constitution of the United States, Judge Story, remarks: "It is notorious that even to this day, in some foreign countries, it is a crime to speak on any subject, religious, philosophical, or political, what is contrary to the received opinions of the Government, or the institutions of the country, however laudable may be the design, and however virtuous may be the motive. Even to animadvert upon the conduct of public men, of rulers, or of representatives, in terms of the strictest truth and courtesy, has been and is deemed a scandal upon the supposed sanctity of their stations and characters, subjecting the party to grievous punishment. In some countries no works can be printed at all, whether of science, or literature, or philosophy, without the previous approbation of the Government; and the press has been shackled, and compelled to speak only in the timid language which the cringing courtier, or the capricious inquisitor has been willing to license for publication. The Bible itself, the common inheritance, not merely of Christendom, but of the world, has been put exclusively under the control of Government; and has not been allowed to be seen, or heard, or read, except in a language unknown to the common inhabitants of the country. To publish a translation in the vernacular tongue, has been in former times a flagrant offence."*

This is an impressive passage, which, like many others that might be pointed out, must, as a legitimate consequence of the exclusion of the Bible and all religious truth from our Common School system, be obliterated from our school literature. The Roman Catholic Church can no more permit the Bible to be

* Story on the Constitution, p. 263.

spoken of as the common inheritance of Christendom and of the world in the volumes of the District School Library, than it can permit the Bible to be read in the common schools. And the theory that there must be no religious bias in the schools will operate with an equally fatal logical destructiveness to the obliteration of thousands of instructive pages in the established common school literature. There can, indeed, be no such thing as freedom in that literature on this theory; and restrictions which Judge Story points out as criminal and disgraceful in other countries, and destructive of the spirit of liberty, would be found realized in this.

It is a true and noble expression, in which Judge Story has characterized the Bible. THE COMMON INHERITANCE OF CHRISTENDOM AND OF THE WORLD. It is an expression that accords with that of the divinely inspired Legislator, when he said: "The things that are revealed belong to us AND TO OUR CHILDREN forever."

The question may be asked, Are the children of Christendom alone,—those gathered in a system of Common School education—to be excluded from the possession and benefit of this inheritance? Are the children,—those persons whom the State designates as entitled to the privileges of an education, say during the period between six years of age and twenty,—a part of Christendom, or does this common inheritance belong only to persons who are not minors? Are they alone to be regarded as capable of this freedom? Must this common inheritance be shut out from the knowledge of all for whom the State undertakes to provide an education, until the period when that education is finished? Or say from the knowledge of those, who have no other schools or teachings than those which the State furnishes, and no means of gaining any other education?

The Common Inheritance of Christendom and of the World!—Then those who would conceal and withdraw it from the world—those who would put it under ban, restraint, imprisonment—those who forbid it to be read, are the common pirates and highway robbers of Christendom and the world. They might,

with as much propriety, dispute the common highway of the seas. The principles embraced in this just view of the universality, supremacy, and freedom of the Bible for all mankind, are fundamental, and of the greatest importance in relation to the claim to governmental and international protection on the part of those who undertake the spreading of the Scriptures. Our country's authority and power may justly be exerted to shield to the uttermost those who are engaged in carrying the Bible to other lands. We may rightfully demand, from all nations, this privilege of freely circulating the Word of God, and that reciprocity of religious liberty which we give to all, and which, by international law, we maintain in the concerns of our commercial policy.

THE COMMON INHERITANCE OF CHRISTENDOM AND OF THE WORLD!—Let not, then, our own free country submit to the exclusion of it, at the instigation of a sect, from the public schools, those foundations of pure and virtuous opinion. Let us not set the example to Christendom and the world, of treating the Bible as a sectarian book, a book that must be

excluded because it is religious and teaches religion, which its adversaries assume that it is no function of the Government to do. But if the Government undertake to provide for the children an education in all things essential to their well-being as citizens, it cannot rightfully omit some provision of knowledge in regard to religion. This may be maintained as an indisputable axiom.

"The right of a society or Government," says Judge Story, "to interfere in matters of religion, will hardly be contested by any persons, who believe that piety, religion, and morality, are intimately connected with the well-being of the State, and indispensable to the administration of civil justice. The promulgation of the great doctrines of religion, the being and attributes and providence of one Almighty God; the responsibility to Him for all our actions, founded upon moral accountability; a future state of rewards and punishments; the cultivation of all the personal, social, and benevolent virtues;—these can never be a matter of indifference in any well-ordered community. It is, indeed, difficult to conceive how any civilized society can well exist without them. And, at all events, it is impossible for those who believe in the truth of Christianity as a Divine revelation, to doubt *that it is the especial duty of Government to foster and encourage it among all the citizens and subjects.* This is a point wholly distinct from that of the right of private judgment in matters of religion and of the freedom of public worship, according to the dictates of one's conscience."*

These sentiments are accordant with those of the wisest statesmen and purest patriots of our country, from the days of Washington to this hour. We could not desire a more complete and explicit description of the kind and degree of religious instruction which may be demanded and expected from the Government in a system of free common school education. The truths on the subject of religion, for the inculcation of which it is the duty of the State to provide in such a system, and for the provision of which, according to Mr. Webster, the State, in undertaking a system

* **Story on the Constitution, p. 260.**

of education, and taxing the people for it, has plighted its faith to all its citizens, are such, that truly, in the language of Judge Story, "it is difficult to conceive how any civilized society can exist without them." They are religious truths, and cannot possibly be taught at all without a religious bias; yet they are not sectarian, nor can any provision against sectarianism be made to touch them, nor any sectarian jealousy rightfully exclude them. Nevertheless, the assumptions in the argument against the Bible in schools would shut them out completely.

Fatal Policy of the Exclusion of Religion.

OPINION OF WASHINGTON, AND OF THE FRAMERS OF THE CONSTITUTION.

THE endeavor to exclude religion and a "religious bias" from our character and policy as a government and a nation, is a dangerous and alarming effort. The exclusion of the Bible from our common school system, on the ground that no "religious bias" should be admitted there, would be a fatal policy. This movement appears in strong and melancholy contrast with the advice of Washington, and with the sentiments and measures of the framers of our country's Constitution. In his Farewell Address, Washington uttered the following warnings: "Of all the dispositions and habits which lead to political prosperity, Religion and Morality are indispensable supports. In vain would that man claim the tribute of patriotism, who should labor to subvert these great pillars of human happiness, these purest props of the duties of men and citizens. The mere politician, equally with the pious man, ought to respect and cherish them. A volume could not trace all their connections with private and public felicity. Let it simply be asked, Where is the security for property, for reputation, for life, if the sense of religious obligation desert the oaths, which are the instruments of investigation in Courts of Justice? And let us with caution indulge the supposition that morality can be maintained without religion. Whatever may be conceded to the influence of refined education on minds of peculiar structure, reason and experience both forbid us to expect that national morality can prevail in exclusion of religious principle."

Now, have our public schools anything to do with our national morality, or have they not? If they have, then how can they be preserved as safe instrumentalities in the formation of our national character and habits, without religious principle, "in exclusion of religious principle"? But what more complete and perfect exclusion of religious principle, than the exclusion of the Bible as a sectarian book? And what could lay a broader foundation for national infidelity and immorality, than such an excommunication of the Word of God?

The opinion of the framers of our Constitution may be known from the following sentence in the fourth article in the ordinance for the government of the North-west Territory. "Religion, morality, and knowledge, being necessary to good government and the happiness of mankind, schools and the means of education shall forever be encouraged." Religion, then, as well as morality and knowledge, was, in the opinion of these statesmen, an end to be accomplished by the schools, and, of course, religion was to be taught in them. Indeed, they were of the same opinion with Washington, that morality itself cannot be maintained without religion. How different from these just sentiments, how opposed to them, is the rule asserted in these modern days, at the instigation of a sect, that an impartial system of public education must be free from any religious bias. What a vast distance from the opinions and feelings of our fathers we must have wandered, to accept of such a canon as the basis of our public schools.

There cannot be such a thing as true religion without a religious bias, nor such a thing as a religious bias without a bias towards religion. The religion which our forefathers contemplated and intended as being taught in the common schools, was certainly not indifference to all religion, nor the treating of all religions as alike, nor the studied and formal rejection of the Word of God. This is not the way to produce a religious influence, nor the way to teach either religion or morality; but it is in speaking of education particularly, that Washington declared, that reason and experience forbid us to expect that national morality can prevail in exclusion of religious principle. But if you have a studied exclusion of everything distinctively religious, if you forbid any religious bias to such a degree as to shut out the Bible itself, on the ground that nothing distinctively religious must be admitted, you render the teaching of religious principle in the schools impossible, you exclude every reference to religion, every acknowledgment of Christianity.

You not only ignore the existence of religious principle, but you guard against it, you fend it off, you mark it as you would a wild beast or a pestilence. The indulgence of a boa-constrictor, or of the small-pox among the children, could not be more jealously forbidden. In this respect, your schools are like an Oriental harem; the very appearance of the slippers of religion indicates the presence of a criminal, and the vigilant eunuchs are upon you with the bow-string—a Roman bow-string for the Bible! Is *this* the condition to which the school system of a generation but one remove from Washington and our revolutionary fathers is to be reduced, at the inquisitorial dictatorship of Romish priests? Free public schools! What a burlesque upon the name of freedom, where the Bible is carefully shut out, where the very Lord's Prayer is branded as intolerance and sectarianism, where the books and the principles which alone can lay the foundation or teach the nature of civil and religious freedom, are interdicted. It would be a suicidal policy for our freedom and our piety, if such a course should be adopted. It would be the most lunatic instance the world has even seen of the madness of digging down the charcoal foundations of the temple, under pretence of providing a universal fuel for the fires upon its altars.

The Essential Requisites in a Common School Education.

CASE OF THE DEAF AND DUMB.

A COMMON school education at the expense of the State would be based upon a wrong principle, if it ignored or excluded any knowledge admitted to be essentially important for all intelligent creatures, everywhere, under all circumstances, as members of the State. A common school education should be such, that whatever is essential to the well-being and good citizenship of the pupil, should be taught there, in its principles at least, should be accessible there, as if no other means of instruction were to be ever in his power. A common school education ought to teach so much of Christianity and the Word of God, that a child could be saved by it, if he never knew any more of it, nor from any other source.

A common school education ought not to rely upon the hope or possibility of anything essential to the well-being and good citizenship of the pupil, being taught anywhere else, and on account of that possibility to exclude that vital element.

There is, in point of fact, a multitude of persons, whose children are never taught religion at home, not even the existence and attributes of God, the laws of moral probation for mankind, nor even the being of a Saviour. They never see a Bible, never hear its lessons, never listen to a verse of it. From such, in legislating the Bible out of schools, from a professed regard to the largest religious liberty, you take away the only opportunity of coming to a knowledge of the nature of Christianity and the Word of God, in the most important and critical of all periods for laying the foundations of the character. It would be treason in the State towards the intelligent and immortal creatures thus thrown upon its care, to withhold from them what is most essential to their welfare.

The amount of immigration alone, into our

country, and of the increase in this way of a population-element needing to be taught, is upwards of four hundred thousand a year. Of what infinite importance that an education which, to say the least, does not ignore and exclude Christianity and the Bible, be given to these! Of what importance that the thousands of children not likely in any other way to become acquainted with the Bible at all, learn something of it in the common school; learn at least that there is such a volume as the Word of God, and know something of the beauty and power of its sacred lessons. It is admitted on all hands that we are in great danger from the dark and stolid infidelity and vicious radicalism of a large portion of the foreign immigrating population. What, then, can be done to ward off this danger, and how can we reach the evil at its roots, applying a wise and conservative radicalism to defeat the working of that malignant, social, anti-Christian poison? How can the children of such a population be reached, except in our free public schools? If the Bible be read in them, its daily lessons cannot but be attended by the

Divine blessing, and in many instances may beget such a reverence for the Word of God, and instil such a knowledge of its teachings, that the infidelity of their home education shall be effectually counteracted. And if the religious influence that prevails in our best school-books be thrown around them, that influence, constant and familiar, though in no respect sectarian, will be as a guiding and transfiguring light in the formation of their opinions and the education of their feelings.

But exclude the Bible from the schools, and accompany that exclusion, as to be logically consistent you must, with a dephlogistication of your school-books, to expurgate from them the whole religious element, and where will the children of this class of our population learn anything better than the gloomy and destructive infidelity of their parents and associates? The Bible does not spring up as a guardian angel in the beer-shops, and the exclusion of the Bible and of all "religious bias" from the common schools is really giving them over into the power of the Tempter, without a solitary warning in their education that can put them on their guard, without an instruction by which they can distinguish between truth and error, without an influence or a weapon of protection or defence.

The State provides for the religious instruction of the deaf and dumb. By what right or authority can it do this, and not be guilty of an intolerant oppression of the consciences of those who do not desire such instruction, if there be not the same right and authority to institute the teaching or reading of the Bible in the common schools? The Institution for the Deaf and Dumb is under the same general laws as the common schools, and the people's money is appropriated for its support; and if a religious bias, or the reading of the Bible, is a wrong to conscience in the public schools, so it is there. But who would dare lift up a voice against that institution of mercy, on the ground that it is sectarian, intolerant, and oppressive to the conscience? Yet it is but a public school; and in regard to all knowledge of the Word of God, many of the children in our streets, who have ears to hear, and tongues to ask and to answer, are as destitute and vacant, and as likely to continue so, if that knowledge be not communicated in the common schools, as if they were in reality both deaf and dumb. Nay, if they were so, and the Bible were excluded from the common schools, while it is admitted into the schools for the instruction of the deaf and dumb, then they they would be far more likely in their misfortune, and by the very means of it, to know the Word of God, and be saved, than if they possessed the common faculties of humanity.

Take now the simple and affecting description of the scenes at the last anniversary of this institution, and say if there was anything in the reported exercises of the pupils that could, even in our common schools, have justly offended any man's conscience. The President of the Institution declared that there is "scarcely a State in the Union of any considerable population and resources, that has not fully or in part acknowledged the claims of this interesting and unfortunate portion of its population to the means of intellectual and spiritual life." Intellectual *and* Spiritual; this is just. But if the deaf and dumb children need the spiritual as well as intellectual, so do all other children thrown upon the State for their education; nay, more, in proportion to the more active part they will be called to take in the affairs of life and of the country. And if the State can, without violation of conscience and of right, give the Bible to deaf and dumb children in their schools, and ought so to do, (which who will deny?) it can and ought, by the same rule, to all the children in the common schools; it would be cruelty and oppression to take it away from these, and favoritism to bestow it upon those. The visitors at this Institution were charmed with the proofs of success in developing the religious sentiment and conscience of the pupils, and delighted at the clearness, simplicity, and promptness of the replies that had been made to questions of a religious import.

"Who made the world?" was the question once proposed to a little boy in the Institution. Without an instant's delay the chalk had rapidly traced the answer:

"In the beginning God created the Heavens and the earth."

"Why did Jesus come into the world?" was the next question proposed. With a smile of gratitude the little fellow wrote in reply:

"This is a faithful saying, and worthy of all acceptation, that Christ Jesus came into the world to save sinners." The astonished visitor, desirous of testing the religious nature of the pupil to the utmost, ventured at length to ask,

"Why were you born deaf and dumb, when I can both hear and speak?" With the sweetest and most touching expression of meek resignation on the face of the boy, the rapid chalk replied:

"Even so, Father, for it seemeth good in thy sight."

Now suppose that such a scene, at a public examination, and as the result of the reading of the Scriptures, had taken place in one of our common schools; who dare pretend or affirm that *that* would be an intrusion upon the rights of conscience, an oppression by the State, of those who reject the Scriptures, or an over-stepping of the proper sphere of government?

Argument from the Nature of an Oath.

THERE is another line of argument to prove unanswerably that the State not only *may* justly interfere to appoint religious instruction to be given in the common schools, but must do so, to be consistent with other statutes and appointments for the people. For example: The State appoints the formality of an oath to be taken on the Bible, for the swearing of witnesses, and on many other occasions; it is a very common administration by the State. Now, if this be anything serious, if it be not the gravest yet most absolute mockery, it is a religious reality of the highest and most solemn import and authority. But *though* a religious reality, still it *is* a mockery, if the State, having appointed this form of oath by law, and provided for its sacredness, do *not* provide the means of understanding it; if the State exclude from the very elements of a common school education, that knowledge, that instruction, by which alone it is possible to understand it. The children of the State should surely be taught what an oath is, if, when they grow up to be citizens, they are liable to have it administered on occasions of the most critical nature and importance.

But simply to teach the nature of an oath, the State must have the power to teach religious truth, and must provide for its being taught in a common school education. For what is the nature of an oath? An appeal to Almighty God, the governor and judge of mankind, an appeal on the ground of the great doctrines of revealed religion that God searches the heart, that we are accountable to him, that he will one day bring us into judgment for every thought, word, and action, and that he will punish the guilty and reward the righteous. How can the nature of an oath be taught, without teaching the sinfulness of a lie before God, and the certainty of his vengeance? How, without teaching that for every idle word that men shall speak, they shall give account in the Day of Judgment? How can the power of an oath be felt, without the knowledge of its sanctions, the knowledge of the truth, and holiness, and justice of Jehovah, the knowledge that if it be falsely taken, all liars are by name excluded from the Kingdom of Heaven, and appointed to the endurance of God's righteous indignation?

Now, these things are religious teachings, most important, most invaluable, for the training of the conscience and the heart; and if the State have any right to command the oath, the State has the same right, and comes under the highest obligation, to provide for and appoint such teachings, that her citizens may know their commonest forms of duty, and be prepared for their sincere and intelligent performance. And what did Washington say upon this very point? Let us recur to the sentence, which he wrote expressly to prove the absolute necessity of religion as well as morality for the existence and well-being of the State, and therefore the necessity of the teaching of religion as well as morality. "Let it be simply asked," said he, "where is the security for property, for reputation, for life, if the sense of religious obligation desert the oaths, which are the instruments of investigation in courts of justice?" But that sense *must* desert them, if men are not taught those religious truths, by which only the oath can be understood in its sacredness, and in the knowledge of which alone it is worth anything. Now, is the State bound to provide means for the preparation of the children for the obligations and duties of a citizen, in taking upon itself the work of their education, or is it not? If any education be given by the State, surely it must be such that by means of it the children may arrive at the knowledge of those obligations and responsibilities which will rest upon them as members of the State. And what an anomaly, what a profound and palpable inconsistency, to appoint and enjoin a religious obligation for our civil and social life, and at the same time enjoin the exclusion from our common schools of all the peculiar instruction and knowledge requisite for performing it! If the State have any authority to prohibit sectarianism in the common schools, it has a still higher authority, and more binding obligation, to provide for the teaching of religious truth. The truths on which an oath is founded, the State *must* teach.

The very last occasion on which Daniel Webster ever appeared in Faneuil Hall, in Boston, he uttered a passage on the nature of the work of a popular education, which deserves to be inscribed over the door of every common school-house in America:—

"We seek to educate the people. We seek to improve men's moral and religious condition. In short, we seek to work upon mind as well as upon matter. And in working on mind, it enlarges the human intellect and the human heart. We know that when we work upon materials, immortal and imperishable, that they will bear the impress which we place upon them, through endless ages to come. If we work upon marble, it will perish; if we work upon brass, time will efface it. If we rear temples, they will crumble to the dust. But if WE WORK ON

MEN'S IMMORTAL MINDS—IF WE IMBUE THEM WITH HIGH PRINCIPLES, WITH THE JUST FEAR OF GOD, AND OF THEIR FELLOW-MEN—WE ENGRAVE ON THOSE TABLETS SOMETHING WHICH NO TIME CAN EFFACE, BUT WHICH WILL BRIGHTEN AND BRIGHTEN TO ALL ETERNITY."

INFIDEL ASPECT AND TENDENCY

OF THE EXCLUSION OF

Religion from a Common School Education.

It has been the conviction of some of the wisest men that ever lived, that an education may be infidel, and therefore immoral, in its tendency, without a shade of positive infidel teaching, by the bare fact of entirely ignoring and excluding Christianity. Certainly, there are no direct moral lessons in mathematics or any of the sciences, unless the light of religion is brought to play upon them. Morality itself, according to the sentiment we have quoted from Washington, is based upon religion, and if religion be excluded, morality is also. The most perfect knowledge of physical law will not restrain the passions; the sanctions of religion are essential for that. But really, to ignore and exclude religion is to teach that it is not necessary, if it be not also directly to teach that there is no such thing, no one true religion, in regard to which there is any certainty that it is the truth, any more than all forms of religion under heaven are the truth. Is there not, must there not be, necessarily, inevitably, an infidel influence in such teaching?

There is power and truth in this declaration. It is not bigotry, it is not attachment to sectarianism, but it is true religious knowledge and feeling, that produces this sentiment, this conviction, on the part of those churches that entertain it; and they are not few. They do believe that where you carefully divorce and exclude all religious teaching from secular teaching, and permit only the last, the inculcation is that of a potential infidelity; and if this becomes a characteristic of our school system, and the grand rule for cutting and drying it, is to be the careful expulsion of the religious element, under politicians for commissioners and superintendents, the churches will not support it, and will refuse to be taxed for it. They will never consent that the Government, merely because it allows the people to tax themselves for free schools, shall set up such a tyrannical expurgation of the Bible and religion from the system of the education of their children.

But here you are prompt to answer, algebra is not infidel; reading, writing, arithmetic, are not infidel; there can be no irreligion in one's A B C's. No! but if to each one of these branches, and to the learning of them, is attached the prohibition, you shall *not* couple with them any religious teaching, you shall *not* read nor teach the Scriptures along with them; this ban of excommunication leaves a positive taint upon the school. The jealousy and exclusion of religion and of the Scriptures attaches unconsciously to all the branches taught under such an interdiction; an instinctive repulsion *is* taught, on the part of all the school exercises, habits, discipline, against religious light and liberty. The pressure of such a negative may not be felt or acknowledged definitely, at present, on any one point; but in the long run, and as a whole, it must be of prodigious and pernicious power. It acts as a standing, perpetual insinuation, argument, and warning, against the Word of God. Taken in connection with a multiplicity of other influences and efforts of infidelity to weaken the hold of the Scriptures on the public mind, the mass of the community will be poorly prepared to withstand the insidious attack. The general voice of the nation will seem to be against the Word of God, and it will be presented in the attitude of an object of the fear and jealousy of the country. This is an effect quite inevitable from any such guarded exclusion of it from a system of free public education; any candid mind must be convinced of this on a moment's reflection. Suppose that in Austria, for example, any copy of the American Constitution, and all allusions to it, and to the system of free government founded upon it, were forbidden in all the schools, so that any teacher who should undertake to enlighten a class concerning it, or to teach the wisdom of its principles, would be subject to an ignominious dismissal from his office; could it be otherwise than that such guarded exclusion should impress a general sense of something dangerous and pernicious in that constitution and system of government? Would it not be passing strange for a people professing a conviction of the supreme excellence of that system, to enact such edicts against it? Could the effect be possibly otherwise than injurious towards it? There are cases in which a studied silence and omission are the greatest reproach.

It is hardly needful to refer to authorities on this subject; it would be superfluous, were it not for the amazing extent to which an anti-Christian sophistry has carried captive a portion of the public mind. "The Christian principles," says John Foster, "cannot be true, without determining what shall be true in the mode of representing all those subjects with which they hold a connection. He who has sent a revelation to declare the theory of sacred truth, and to order the relations of all moral sentiments with that truth, cannot give his sanction at once to this final constitution, and to that which disowns it. God therefore disowns that, which disowns the religion of

Christ, and what he disowns he condemns, thus placing all moral sentiments in the same predicament, with regard to the Christian economy, in which Jesus Christ placed his contemporaries, 'He that is not with me, is against me.'"

"An *entire* separation of moral science" (and consequently of education) "from religion it is hardly possible to preserve, since Christianity has decided some moral questions on which reason was dubious or silent; and since that final retribution which the New Testament has so luminously foreshown, is evidently the greatest of sanctions. To make *no* reference, while inculcating moral principles, to a judgment to come, after that judgment has been declared on what has been confessed to be divine authority, would look like systematic irreligion."

But any reference to such truths, or inculcation of such lessons, produces a religious bias, and is the inculcation of distinctively religious truth, though not sectarian. And if God disowns that which disowns religion, he must disown a system of education which rejects it from the things to be taught, defrauds the mind of its sanctions, and places the creature in a state of constant exile from the climate of the kingdom of Christ. It walls off the thoughts from all contact with the eternal realities of our being, and naturalizes the mind to an existence like a dungeon. The unfortunate objects of such a discipline of jealousy against religious truth, remind us of one of Foster's illustrations; "they are somewhat like the inhabitants of those towns within the vast salt mines of Poland, who, beholding every object in their region by the light of lamps and candles only, have in their conversation no expressions describing things in such aspects as never appear but under the lights of heaven."

Now, connect with this such an extract as you may make almost at random from the annual reports of any of our benevolent societies, designed for the good of children, and of the poor, as, for example, the last report of the Association of New York, stating the condition of multitudes of children, who are taught nothing of God, nothing of Divine truth, nothing of the Saviour of the world, nothing but vagrancy, low cunning, and vice; and suppose a multitude of such children gathered into a school, from which all reference to religion, all religious distinctive instruction, all lessons from Divine truth in regard to God, and the relations of man to the future world, as a world of retribution and reward; and if they get no education but such as the State gives them in such a school, in what better condition would they be, as respects "the lights of heaven," than that of the inhabitants of the mines of Poland?

Strange delusion, to think of benefiting the children of the poor and vicious, by bringing them into schools under the rule of a studied exclusion of the Bible, and all religious instruction; a system of education properly described as wearing the stamp of systematic irreligion! Yet such is precisely the course of policy to which this community are urged, on the plea of accommodating the school system to the conscience of a sect, the maintenance of whose power depends on keeping the Bible from their children, and their children from the knowledge of the Bible!

Argument from the Necessity of Religious Self-government.

I HAVE at this moment lying before me a discourse by a popular preacher, reported in one of our public papers, in which it it proclaimed that in our country, the foundation of power in the individual and liberty in the masses is self-government, founded on religious belief and conscience; the necessity is forcibly and eloquently presented, of "religious inspiration and religious self-control in the individual," and it is declared that "if these be lost or corrupted, our expiring anguish will surpass that of any nation that ever lived." This position may be completely maintained; it is almost a truism concerning the nature of republican freedom, that it is impossible without the habit of self-government. But who ever heard of religious inspiration and religious self-control without the knowledge of the Word of God? And where shall this sense and knowledge of religion and of the Scriptures, presented as of such vital importance to the preservation of our country's liberties, be taught? Can it be safely left to the churches, and to those schools where sectarian tenets are taught? The answer instantly presents itself that, as a general rule, the churches and those schools are patronized or frequented by those only, or mainly, who have the Bible taught in their families, and that, moreover, there are not enough of such churches and schools to accommodate a fourth—no, not an eighth-part of the community.

The argument in behalf of the very existence of free public schools, is an argument for the necessity of the Bible in them. The churches and the parochial schools are glaringly inadequate; perhaps not more than a sixth part of the families in our country ever attend any church, or any other schools than the free schools. Consequently, five-sixths of our whole youthful population are left unprovided with the knowledge of the Bible and any religious instruction, if you exclude it from the free public schools. Consequently, if it be so excluded, the very idea of it will come to five-sixths of our children only as a thing to be guarded against, and of which they know little else but this only, that it is forbidden in the public schools. Nor would this interdiction be particularly likely to make them inquire for it elsewhere.

The inconsistency of such a course is manifest. Our whole possibility of safety and prosperity as a country is founded on habits and influences of religious self-control, and yet, the only book that teaches such control without sectarianism, and provides the elements for it, forbidden in the *free* public schools, and shut out from the knowledge of five-sixths of the people's children! Language cannot state strongly enough the grossness of this inconsistency, nor the greatness of the danger from such a course. Then, too, the evil which needs to be diminished, of such a rivalry between private schools and the free school system, as places them at antagonism, and presents the private schools as the more moral, more respectable, more select and safe, both for the mind and heart, the manners and morals of the pupil,—that evil would be greatly increased; for any parent of sane and unprejudiced mind would prefer, though at far greater cost, to send a child to school where the Word of God is free, and religious instruction at least is possible.

If you undertake to educate all the children of the State, to bring them all together in harmony, in one and the same grand system, that all may have the advantages of each, and each of all, that every division may be avoided which has the effect of placing one portion of the children in a higher and better system, and another less favored portion in a poorer and more limited system; if you would thus dispense with the necessity of particular and private schools, for those who are not satisfied with the governmental schools, because they do but half educate the child, in educating the mind only; then must you combine, in your common school system, all the requisites for a thorough education of the whole being. You cannot leave out the moral and religious element, and satisfy the people; they will not long, nor unitedly, sustain a system with so glaring and radical a deficiency. If you would provide an education for all, and equally, then must you *level up*, not *down*.

If you demand that the private and parochial schools shall throw away their Bible, and its precious religious truth, its sacred lessons, merely to give a grander support to your schools *without* the Bible, your schools *divorced* from religion, and *excluding* it, you will demand in vain; you can find no such patriotism as *that* in the Church of Christ in America. If you divorce your schools from the Bible and religion, you will divorce them from the affections, the respect, the support, and the patronage of Christians; and so divorced, the common school system cannot stand. They who love the Bible will not consent to have the education of their children levelled down, to meet the merely secular and contracted standard of those who exclude it.. They who believe and declare that the freedom of religious truth alone can render an education truly free and comprehensive, will never consent to put their children under a system of jealousy, restraint, and fear, in the presence of Divine truth, and in the guarded exclusion of it.

It is singular to see, in the same breath, an utterance of the conviction, or professed conviction, that it is to the supremacy of religious principle and religious truth in the minds and hearts of our fathers that we owe the birth and establishment of our admirable institutions of civil and religious liberty; that it was their sense of dependence upon God, and their earnest seeking of Divine guidance, and their deep impression of the same principles on their children, that rendered those institutions, or could alone render them, permanent;—and then an utterance of contempt or of serious argument against the Bible and religious instruction in our schools, just as if there were no more connection between our future prosperity and the truth by which our fathers prospered, than between the harvest which was reaped a hundred years ago, and that which we confidently believe will cover the hill-sides of New England next year. Have we arrived at such a religious state, are we so permeated already with the knowledge and the influence of religion, that the process of instruction in divine truth may safely stop, the Bible be turned out of school, and religion exorcised from the common school education, as a superfluous or intruding visitor with whom we have no longer any necessary concern?

It is admitted that we owe our present high prosperity, our good order, our civil and religious freedom, to the knowledge and influence of the Bible among all classes. And can we now afford to throw down the ladder, by which we have ascended to these blessings, and leave others to gain them as they may? Can we safely rely upon an uninstructed generation to keep them, or even to appreciate their value? Or is there really such an indefatigable and all-conquering zeal for teaching religion to the children of the masses out of school, as will supply the want of it in the common school education?

Illustrations from Scotland.

ARGUMENT BY DR. CANDLISH.—OPINION OF BUNSEN.

MR. GLADSTONE of England recently declared, in speaking of the happy union of religious and secular instruction in the schools in Scotland, that there is the closest and the happiest harmony between the scientific training of the intellect and the religious training of the heart; that he commits a profanation against God and against human nature who would attempt to dissever them; and that where the truths of the Christian faith are fully taught and rightly received, there you will best and most fruitfully pursue the work of that temporal and secular training, which is the specific object of the school. In the acknowledgment and light of the Christian faith, and not in the exclusion of it, that specific object is to be pursued; for surely one specific result, if not design, of a school from which the Christian religion is by law excluded, will be the product of infidelity.

Dr. Candlish, in speaking recently in Edinburgh, on the importance of retaining the religious element in the common schools, established the point that that element may be introduced without sectarianism, and without offence to any conscience. The children were permitted to avail themselves of the religious instruction in the schools or not according to the pleasure of their parents; but it was found that the Roman Catholics themselves chose the whole course. "Dr. Candlish then showed the non-sectarian character of the education given in the schools, as indicated by the fact that it appeared from the returns of 568 of the schools, that there were in these schools 31,999 scholars whose parents belonged to the Free Church, 10,054 belonging to the Established Church, 614 Roman Catholics, and 9,223 belonging to other denominations. It is a principle of our scheme, said Dr. Candlish, as I believe it is generally in schools in Scotland, that parents may withdraw their children from religious instruction altogether. They may avail themselves of any one branch of education, and decline to avail themselves of any other branch. That liberty is conceded in most schools in Scotland. I think it a proper principle, and one which greatly facilitates the right settlement of the question. Of the 618 Roman Catholics attending our schools, I have not learned an instance—and I do not believe there is one—of an application for the exemption of their children from religious instruction. I believe they generally conform to the whole course of education, unless some priest comes over from the land of intolerance with fresh zeal. But be that as it may. The second statement I have to make on this point is this:—We selected 75 schools in the large towns of Scotland, and found that there were in them 4,658 children of parents belonging to the Free Church, 1,904 belonging to the Established Church, 212 Roman Catholics, and 3,357 of other denominations—in all, 4,658 of Free Church children, and 5,487, or a considerable majority, belonging to other denominations; so that our scheme manifestly bears on the face of it the character of thorough catholicism, thorough unsectarianism."

This is a most important and impressive testimony; and not less important, and applicable to our own case, is the principle justly laid down by Dr. Candlish, that as to the matter of religious instruction, the Scottish educational traditions and hereditary principles of education ought to be regarded; "it was the right of the Scottish people, for there were such hereditary educational principles in Scotland, as made it easy to bring in a system of education that would harmonize all, and place education on a religious, and yet non-sectarian basis. There ought to be, in Scotland, a national system, and that system ought to be, according to the hereditary traditions of Scotland, the use and wont of Scotland, in educational matters, since Scotland was a reformed country."

Now, in regard to ourselves, this right is still clearer and more positive. The hereditary educational principle with us always has been the Bible at the foundation, and religious instruction *from* the Bible. It is no new thing. The innovation would be the exclusion of the Bible, a tyrannical defiance and destruction of all our usages from the outset, at the demand of a single sect. The Bible in the schools has been the custom and common law of the schools from their origin. The Bible ousted *from* the schools is a new and oppressive law sought to be forced upon us by a particular political and ecclesiastical party. We have the right of our forefathers, and of habit and law from the beginning downwards, as well as the right of God and duty, for the Bible in the schools; and none shall take it from us. Dr. Candlish would have the question so settled in Scotland (and it is the right view) as that it shall not be in the power of local boards so much as to raise the question whether there shall be religious teaching; there always has been, and it ought not to be in the power of any to say that there shall not be. "Let there be exceptional cases, if you choose, but surely, the national mind of Scotland being clear, all but unanimous, it will be a grievous hardship, a gross outrage, if we be hindered from getting a settlement of the national question on that footing, or be forced into a settlement of the question on a footing that shall leave out the whole matter of religion, by some scruples in certain quarters about the recognition in an Act of Parliament that there should be religious teaching, and that it should be conducted in the manner hitherto in use."

Dr. Candlish then declares his fear that we are on the eve of a very serious struggle as regards education; and he goes on to bear testimony against the views of those who would exclude the Bible and all religious bias, and would base the system of education solely on the broad principles of "secularism." He refers to some productions by those gentlemen, and then says, that it "seems to be the faith of those parties that the mere knowledge of the physical laws of nature will secure the moral and social well-being of this great community. That radical error runs through all the productions to which I have referred. There seems to be a fixed belief in the minds of those men, that simply to know the physical laws of nature, the laws that regulate demand and supply, is sufficient,—in short, that physics and political economy are enough to secure the social and moral well-being of the community. In the face of such announcements as these, I do humbly think that even some of our friends who have difficulties about the action of the State in religious matters, might pause a little in this question of national education, and consider whether, in these circumstances, and in the view of these influences, it might not be well to have all the security which a most thorough recognition of the religious element can give, that the rising generation shall not be left to the tender mercies of those who would teach them physics and political econony, and say that it is enough to make them good citizens and good men."

The evil and the danger here referred to are precisely the same with those against which we were warned by the foresight of Washington, when he said that we could not hope for the permanence and success of our institutions, in the exclusion of religious principle from our systems of education. It was the voice of a wise, discerning, and sincere patriotism, and no sectarian prejudice; for who will dare accuse Washington of sectarianism or intolerance, in his farewell address to his countrymen?

In this connection the words of the Chevalier Bunsen are worthy to be quoted. The nations of the present age, says Bunsen, "want not less religion, but more:" they want it "to reform the social relations of life, beginning with the domestic, and culminating in the political; an honest *bona fide* foundation, deep as the human mind, and a structure free and organic as nature. This aim cannot be attained without national efforts, CHRISTIAN EDUCATION, free institutions, and social reforms. Then no zeal will be called Christian which is not hallowed by charity, no faith Christian which is not sanctioned by reason. Christianity enlightens now only a small portion of the globe, but it cannot be stationary, it will advance, and is already advancing, triumphantly over the whole earth, in the name of Christ, and in the light of the spirit."*

* Hyppolitus and his age, vol. 2, p. 116.

Mr. Gladstone said, speaking of Scotsmen, and the natural poverty of their country, and the effect of education in placing Scotland in a position among nations second to no other; three or four hundred years ago, they were a nation in the rear of Europe; they are now in front, in the van. The reason for this prodigious and astonishing change was to be found in the fact, that for two centuries the people of Scotland had had the advantage of schools far beyond any other country, far beyond England; and every laboring man in Scotland had had the means of sending his children to them.

But they were not schools destitute of religious bias; if they had been without the Scriptures, in vain would they have been instituted. They, no more than the schools of New England, founded by our Puritan Ancestors, were left without the Bible; and it is to the Bible in schools, high and low, common and select, that Scotland, as well as New England, owes her high position. Her independent rugged peasantry, and the inhabitants of her mountain homes, would never otherwise have maintained their unconquered and unconquerable religious patriotism, their spirit of civil and religious liberty.

In this connection the interesting fact may be named, relative to the advancing character and position of the Sandwich Islands, wholly based from the outset on the Word of God, that at an early period the teachers of the common schools finding a deficiency of school-books, and that the New Testament was the cheapest as well as the best class-book they could employ, adopted that universally; and to the powerful redeeming and enlightening influence thus daily exerted, the rapidly improving character and increasing attainments of the children were to be attributed.

Miss Edgworth tells us that formerly there existed a law in Scotland, which obliged every farrier who, through ignorance or drunkenness pricked a horse's foot in shoeing him, to deposit the price of the horse until he was sound, to furnish the owner with another, and in case the horse could not be cured, the farrier was doomed to indemnify the injured owner. At the same rate of punishment, asks Miss Edgworth, what indemnification should be demanded from a careless or ignorant preceptor?*

We may add, suppose that he had neglected to fasten the nails so that the first hard piece of road the horse had to travel, his shoes would be knocked off, and his feet made incurably lame for want of protection. The security of good principles is what we want in education, and it can be found only in the religion of the Bible; and that system which neglects or wilfully refuses to provide those fastenings, the nails of divine truth, is justly chargable with all the consequences.

* Practical Education, vol. 1. p. 202.

Presentation of the Subject by John Foster.

In arguing with characteristic energy and power for a scheme of popular education, John Foster argues with equal power that religious instruction should form a material part of it. He exposes the miserable absurdity of the plan of divorcing education from religion, and teaching the latter as a separate thing. He shows the importance, the duty, of combining religious with other information, and thus rendering it familiar and natural, a companion of every-day life, and not a formalistic god, or influence of Sundays only, or of Sunday schools. Religion must not be forced upon the mind, or presented by itself as a mere catechetical speculation or abstraction, but must be a daily companion of other more attractive knowledge, because it requires so much care and address to present it in an attractive light; and it is desirable to combine it with other subjects naturally more engaging, and with associations that are most familiar and pleasing to the thoughts.

The question being how to bring the people by the ordinary means of education to a competent knowledge of religious truth, we have to consider the fittest way. "And if," says Foster, "in attentively studying this, there be any who come to ascertain that the right expedient is a bare illustration of religious instruction, disconnected, one system, from the illustrative aid of other knowledge, divested of the modification and attraction of associated ideas derived from subjects less uncongenial with the natural feelings, they really may take the satisfaction of having ascertained one thing more, namely, that human nature has become at last so mightily changed, that it may be left to work itself right very soon, as to the affair of religion, with little further trouble of theirs."

While, therefore, this great writer insists upon the mental cultivation of the masses by all means, at all hazards, accounting all knowledge as being absolutely valuable, an apprehension of things as they are, and tending to prevent delusion, and to remove the obstacles, some of them at least, in the way of right volitions; yet he maintains that never, in any case, should knowledge be separated from religious truth.

"We are not heard," says he, "insisting on the advantages of increased knowledge and mental invigoration among the people, *unconnected with the inculcation of religion.* The zealous friends of popular education consider religion (besides being itself the primary and infinitely the most important part of knowledge) as *a principle indispensable for securing the full benefit of all the rest.* It is desired and endeavored, that the understanding of these opening minds may be taken possession of by just and solemn ideas of their relation to the Eternal, Almighty Being; that they may be taught to apprehend it as an awful reality, that they are perpetually under His inspection; and, as a certainty, that they must at length appear before Him in judgment, and join, in another life, the consequences of what they are in spirit and conduct here. It is to be impressed on them that his will is the supreme law; that his declarations are the most momentous truth known on earth; and his favor and condemnation the greatest good and evil. And it is wished and endeavored to be by the light of this divine wisdom, that they are disciplined in other parts of knowledge; so that nothing they learn may be detached from all sensible relation to it, or have a tendency contrary to it. Thus it is sought to be secured, that as the pupil's mind grows stronger, and multiplies its resources, and he therefore has necessarily more power and means for what is wrong, there may be luminously presented to him, as if celestial eyes visibly beamed upon him, the most solemn ideas that can enforce what is right."

Now, let us take the brief description of such an education presented by Foster, as an approximation towards the only true ideal of a *just* education, an education which the State that undertakes to educate, is pledged to provide for its children, and let us ask if there be anything in it that can rightly be charged as sectarian, or excluded on that ground? Rather, is not an education of the conscience, in all knowledge, under the fear of God, and with a constant reference to Him, the most certain way to prevent sectarianism, and to bring together all the members of such a school, under such a discipline, as children of one common Parent, united in Him?

"Such is the discipline meditated," continues Foster, "for preparing the children to pursue their individual welfare, and act their part as members of the community. They are to be trained in early life to diligent employment of their faculties, tending to strengthen them, regulate them, and give their possessors the power of effectually using them. They are to be exercised to form clear, correct notions, instead of crude, vague, delusive ones. During this progress, and in connection with many of its exercises, their duty is to be inculcated on them in the various forms in which they will have to make a choice between right and wrong in their conduct towards society. There will be reiteration of lessons on justice, prudence, inoffensiveness, love of peace, estrangement from the counsels and leagues of vain and bad men; hatred of disorder and violence, a sense of the necessity of authoritative public institutions to prevent these evils, and respect for them, while honestly administered to this end. All this is to be taught, in many instances directly, in others by reference to confirmation, from the Holy Scriptures, from which authority, will also be impressed, all the while, the principles of religion. And religion, while its grand concern is with the state of the soul towards God and eternal interests, yet takes every principle and rule of morals under its peremptory sanction; making the primary obligation and responsibility be towards God, of everything that is a duty with respect to men. So that, with the subjects of this education, the sense of *propriety* shall be *conscience;* the consideration of how they ought to be regulated in their conduct, as a part of the community, shall be the recollection that their Master in heaven dictates the laws of that conduct, and will judicially hold them amenable for every part of it."

"And is not a discipline thus addressed to the purpose of fixing religious principles in ascendency, as far as that difficult object is within the power of discipline, and of infusing a salutary tincture of them into whatever else is taught, the right way to bring up citizens faithful to all that deserves fidelity in the social compact?"*

* Foster on Popular Ignorance, c. 3.

Argument from the Nature of Moral Science.

THE simplest elements of Moral Science cannot be taught without a religious bias. It is impossible to ignore or exclude Christianity, or place it on the same level with false religions, treating all alike, and at the same time instruct the pupil in the truths of moral philosophy. If you would make the subject of morals a subject of study at all in the common schools, you are absolutely compelled to make choice of some system; and unless you take the remnants of Pagan philosophy for a text-book, you must go upon the ground of Christianity; and you cannot advance a step without breaking that law of impartiality, by which it is asserted, that the State can have nothing to do with religious instruction, but is bound to reject the Bible, and all distinctively religious truth. Morality itself, cannot possibly be taught without distinctively religious truth, so that this alleged rule of impartiality would exclude morality as well as religion from the common schools.

As an illustration of this, we will merely take, from the Course of Instruction in the Central High School, in Philadelphia, one single section among many, of questions at a semi-annual examination, the matter of the section being moral science. The pupil is required to state what is Conscience, and to prove its supremacy with the effect of habit on moral actions, and the respects in which the moral constitution of man is observed to be imperfect, and how those defects are to be remedied.

Division A; *Prof. Kirkpatrick.*—1. What is meant by ethics, and how is the science divided?—2. What is meant by the terms relations and obligations, as used in your text-book?—3. What are the principal relations existing between God and man?—4. Explain the rights and obligations arising from those relations.—5 Prove the existence of a conscience.—6. What is meant by natural religion?—7. Explain the relations existing between natural and revealed religion.—8. How may we learn our duty from the doctrine of general consequences?—9. How may we learn our duty from natural religion, or the light of nature?—10. How may we learn our duty from the Scriptures?

Now, unless, for the sake of excluding all religious bias, we teach a *false* system of morals in the public schools, the merest outline of any *true* system will show that it is absolutely impossible to teach morality, without at the same time teaching a distinctive religion; and this is impossible, without a direct religious bias.

It seems almost superfluous to dwell in detail on this argument. And yet, a plausible sophistry has been so widely spread, and the right of Government to administer a system of education at all, either moral or religious, is so stoutly denied in some quarters, that it becomes necessary. The objection from the danger of sectarianism is thus presented and disposed of by Dr Humphrey, the former

President of Amherst College, in a lecture before the American Institute of Instruction:

"There is, I am aware, in the minds of some warm and respectable friends of popular education, an objection against incorporating religious instruction into the system, as one of its essential elements. It cannot, they think, be done without bringing in along with it the evils of sectarianism. If this objection could not be obviated, it would, I confess, have great weight in my own mind. It supposes that if any religious instruction is given, the distinctive tenets of some particular denomination must be inculcated. But is this at all necessary? Must we either exclude religion altogether from our common schools, or teach some one of the various creeds which are embraced by as many different sects in the ecclesiastical calendar? Surely not. There are certain great moral and religious principles, in which all denominations are agreed, such as the ten commandments, our Saviour's golden rule, everything, in short, which lies within the whole range of duty to God and duty to our fellow-men. I should be glad to know what sectarianism there can be in a schoolmaster's teaching my children the first and second tables of the moral law—to 'love the Lord their God with all their heart, and their neighbor as themselves'—in teaching them to keep the Sabbath holy, to honor their parents, not to swear, nor drink, nor lie, nor cheat, nor steal, nor covet. Verily, if this is what any mean by sectarianism, then the more we have of it in our common schools, the better. 'It is a lamentation, and shall be for a lamentation,' that there is so little of it. I have not the least hesitation in saying, that no instructor, whether male or female, ought ever to be employed, who is not both able and willing to teach morality and religion in the manner which I have just alluded to. Were this faithfully done in all the primary schools of the nation, our civil and religious liberties, and all our blessed institutions, would be incomparably safer than they are now. The parent who says, I do not send my child to school to learn religion, but to be taught reading, and writing, and grammar, knows not "what manner of spirit he is of." It is very certain that such a father will teach his children anything but religion at home; and is it right that they should be left to grow up as heathens in a Christian land? If he says to the schoolmaster, I do not wish you to make my son an Episcopalian, a Baptist, a Presbyterian, or a Methodist, very well. This is not the schoolmaster's business. He was not hired to teach sectarianism. But if the parent means to say, I do not send my child to school to have you teach him to fear God, and keep his commandments, to be temperate, honest and true, to be a good son and a good man, then the child is to be pitied for having such a father; and with good reason might we tremble for all that we hold most dear, if such remonstrances were to be multiplied and to prevail."

It is argued by Romanists that there can be no greater fallacy than to suppose that because it is for the interest of the State that its citizens should be enlightened and virtuous, therefore it is the duty or business of the State to make them wise and virtuous by education. Romanism would gladly, were it possible, take this right and duty from the State, and vest it only in the Priests; and then, and thus, the children might universally be kept in darkness, and Romanism might prevail.

Objection that the Romanists are Excluded, Answered.

But here the objector meets us, and assumes that if the Bible be *not* excluded, the Romanists will, and that the Bible had better be shut out, than the Romanists shut out. To this it would be sufficient to say, that if the Bible *be* excluded, a vastly greater number who require the Bible, and have an unquestionable right to it, will be shut out, and that the Bible had better be admitted, than the friends of the Bible be excluded. Those who demand the Bible are ten to one compared with those who reject it; and those who would be conscientiously excluded from the schools, if the Bible were excluded, are at least five to one, compared with those who would be driven away by its admission. Yet the insulting demand for its exclusion is a demand that for the sake of gratifying *one* million, and gathering in a portion of their children into schools from which religion is driven out, you shall disregard the rights of *ten* millions, and compel them either to establish other schools, or else to submit to an education for *their* children, from which the Bible and religious truths are expelled. Shall the two millions who reject the Bible, rule the twenty who require it, and shall the rights of the twenty be sacrificed to meet the prejudices of the two, or shall the vast and overwhelming majority be permitted to retain the Bible, without injury to the rights of any? Shall a very small minority be admitted to spoil an education for the majority, or shall the vast majority be admitted to vitalize and perfect an education for themselves and for all who will avail themselves of it? Shall the conscience of the majority or that of the minority rule? We have already settled that question.

There are two false assumptions in the objection; first, that if the Bible be *not* excluded the Romanists will be shut out; and second, that if the Bible *be* excluded, you can in that way induce them to come in. They will neither be shut out by admitting the Bible, nor will they be drawn in by excluding the Bible. They wish, indeed, to get the Bible out, and so to do the schools all the injury in their power; but those who oppose the Bible have no intention of supporting the free school system at any rate. The *Bible* of the schools is not the source of their objection to them, but the *freedom* of the schools, and the intermingling of Romish and Protestant children, in such a manner as to break down these barriers of cast and prejudice, by which a church-despotism is so powerfully sustained. Their effort against the Bible is but a battering-ram or Roman *Testudo*, under cover of which they advance against the whole system, and mean to break it up.

Besides, the Romanists are *not* shut out, in any case, but have perfect freedom of admission, if they will. If Haman and Mordecai are both invited to the king's feast, and if Haman, coming to the door, finds that Mordecai is to be one of the guests, and indeed sees him just entering on the other side of the way, and retires in a huff, saying, I will not be present at the same feast with Mordecai, nor eat salt with him, whose fault is it? Who makes the exclusion? Can he justly say that the king has shut him out, because Mordecai was invited? It is his own angry, envious, and inimical feelings that have shut him out; and was it the duty of the king to legislate in behalf of those injurious feelings, or to set up new sumptuary regulations to please his malice? Are hatred and prejudice proper things to be fostered and protected by legislation, which, at the same moment that it protects and sustains the prejudice, legislates *against* those who happen to be its unfortunate objects.

Moreover, let us next see what use the Romanists themselves would make of this exclusion. They demand the Bible to be shut out, on the pretence that it is a bad book, a sectarian book, a Protestant book. Accordingly, you put the excommunicating brand upon it, and shut it out. What language does that prohibition speak to the children? What will the Romish parents and the priests say to the youthful members of their flocks, when they desire to guard them against the Bible? What could they ask, for argument against it, better than this fact, that it is not permitted to be read or taught in schools? My children, they may say, it stands to reason, that if the Bible were a good book, they who tell you that it is, would permit it to be taught to their children. But the Protestants themselves have shut it out; *they* do not suffer it to be read, and of course it cannot be fit to be read. A book of their own, which even the Protestants excommunicate, must be a bad book indeed! Never touch it!

Then again, to others they will say, Behold these godless schools! These Protestants have a religion, which they have the impudence to assert is better than ours, and yet they dare not teach it to their children! It can surely not be deemed very sacred by those, who on considerations of expediency, consent to keep it from their children, consent to excommunicate it from the public schools. Godless, atheistic, worthless! We will have nothing to do with such an education; we cannot, and will not, send our children to such places! And here they would find not a few of every faith, who would join with them. For what parent, who reverences the Word of God, and believes in the vital importance of its religious instructions, would consent to send his children to schools, from which the Word of God, and all religious instruction, are carefully, zealously, and by legislation excluded?

But now as to the reality. Facts have already shown, and daily prove, both in this country, and in Scotland, and in Prussia, that many Romish children will still go to the schools with the Bible in them; and would not go any more frequently or willingly with the Bible out of them; and surely, if we could get one-half educated *with* the Bible, it were better than the whole without. Milton said truly that God cares more for the complete training and growth of one virtuous person, than the restraint of ten vicious. Restraint is all that we can hope for *without* the Scriptures; no religious principle is possible, but with and by *them*. The theory and legislation that reject them, must, to be consistent, reject all religious bias, all religious teaching. This would be to act upon the principle of doing evil that good may come; nay, far worse than even that; it would be doing evil (for certainly the withholding of the Bible and of religious instruction from the young is doing evil: he that withholdeth *corn*, the people shall curse him; how much more he that steals the bread of life from the children), I say it would be doing evil, that an evil prejudice may not be offended, but gratified; and in order that a very few, comparatively, may be kept from contact with the Word of God, who hate that Word, it is doing the evil of keeping vast multitudes from it, who desire and need it. Under pretence of alluring the Romish children into the common schools by excluding the Bible, you are just snatching the Bread of Life from the millions of youthful hands held out for it, in order to gratify the comparative few who wish to be without it.

But, after all, it is not so much a jealousy against the Word of God, that instigates this exclusive policy, as it is the unwillingness of Romanists to have their children mingle freely with the children of Protestants, in the same education, under the same religious light. While all other denominations lay aside their sectarian prejudices at the door of the school-house, and rejoice to mingle as one family under the same light of God's Word, the Roman Catholic sect alone carry *their* sectarian prejudices *into* the school-house, and would force all others into a compliance with their rule. The truth is, they are opposed to such a common school education as threatens to break down the barriers of sect, and of priestly and canon law, and to mingle the children of all persuasions in one family, under one common religious light. Our common free school system does this, and therefore they oppose it.

But in some cases the experiment of exorcising the spirit of religion to accommodate the demands of Romanism, *has been made* on the very plea of being able thus to induce the Romanists to patronize the schools, and has utterly failed; but other and disastrous consequences have *not* failed. An Evening Free

School had been for some years established in Salem. On the plea that Romanists would not attend if there were any religious influence or instruction connected with the school, such influence was given up and excluded. "The school has been conducted in the same manner as previously, excepting that all religious exercises have been dispensed with, in order that the children of Roman Catholic parents might be free to attend. *This change failed of producing the desired effect*, our (Roman) Catholic brethren having provided instruction for their own children. But, on other grounds, it was deemed very proper and advisable. Religious exercises are not understood by the class of youth attending such schools, and if not understood, they are commonly turned to ridicule, and that is infinitely worse than their entire omission."

And yet, the class of youth attending such schools, are stated to be "poor neglected boys and girls, whose circumstances of poverty and work would not allow them to attend day schools." And of such persons it is asserted that religious exercises cannot be understood!

Two hundred and sixteen boys, from thirteen to sixteen years of age! and yet not able to understand religion! and, therefore, the conclusion is that religion must not be taught! Instead of arguing from their ignorance, destitution, and want of *all* instruction elsewhere, that compassion towards them so much the more requires a religious influence, and some religious instruction *there,* the argument is deliberately offered, that they cannot understand religious exercises! And perhaps, too, they cannot understand arithmetic; but is that a reason for not teaching it? Perhaps they do not even understand reading; but is that sufficient reason for not teaching them their letters? If they cannot understand religious exercises, so much the more reason for beginning, in some way, to teach them. But this reasoning, and the disastrous result of turning religion out of school, all proceeds from the first false step of excluding religious exercises, in the vain hope of securing the patronage of Romanists. This is likely to be the result of all such efforts.

Appropriateness and Beauty of the Word of God in our Common Schools.

THE potent energy of God's word as an element of regeneration and transfiguration, both for the intellectual and moral nature, as well as the certainty of the Divine blessing attending its presence, and its constant power, must have been forgotten, if not denied, by those who would exclude it from a place in our system of Common School Education. As an element of quiet, but effectual government and order in the schools, it would be invaluable; where its influence is judiciously employed, by a teacher whose heart loves it, punishment is but seldom needed. It is a forcible preventing, as well as reforming element, yet ever gentle, instructive, and persuasive. What an agency of power, kindness, and love, is foregone, neglected, rejected, when the Bible is excluded from the system of instruction and discipline in school. And what a delightful and attractive variety, in both the form and material of thought, feeling, and imagination, in history, parable, poetry, argument and precept, in the lessons prepared by the Great Teacher of mankind, and given to our race under the gracious perpetual sanction of our birth-right from heaven, with the assurance that the things that are revealed belong to us and to our children forever!

That from a child thou hast known the Holy Scriptures, is the most marked and explicit record of an educational process, as sanctioned of God. Doubtless, it ought to be the process with every immortal being in a Christian State; and it might be, with nearly every one, if the State performed its full responsibility. And when we think of that responsibility as extending, in the course of a few years, to the children of more than a hundred millions, who will at once, within the limits of another generation, be the inhabitants of our country, and think of all those children, during the whole period of their education undertaken by the State, as deprived of the Word of God with all its hallowing and sanctifying influences, its wondrous winning and perpetual power of sacred training and restraint, we regard with amazement the heedlessness, not to say recklessness of consequences, with which any man can deliberately and earnestly propose and labor for the exclusion of that Divine agency from the whole circle of an education so vast and important.

To think how great and beneficial an influence is exerted during the period of one year, in a single district school, by the falling of the Word of God, as the gentle dew from Heaven, in the hushed stillness of the school, morning and evening, on so many opening and susceptible minds and hearts; and then to think of the possibility of making that the reverent habit of the schools of twenty millions; and then to think of that influence carried forward from year to year, as uninterrupted as the rising and setting of the sun, through a period of thirty years, when the children of a population of more than two hundred millions may be thus gathered beneath the same Divine Hand, the same beneficent impression! How imposing, how majestic, how delightful the sight of the children of a whole nation, every day silently listening, at the same hour, to the words of their Father in Heaven, and uniting at the same hour in the petition, Our Father! To think that this might be, was in likelihood of being, and then to conceive the plan of thwarting this possibility, and to labor by argument and management for preventing it! Does it seem possible that such an effort can co-exist with Christian principle? Are the two compatible?

In this connection, how strikingly and solemnly beautiful are the words of John Foster, in reference to the inestimable value of the union of religious truth with secular instruction, and the security and happiness of the mind advancing forward to the responsibilities of life, and the command of thought and action, under such a discipline. He imagines a visitor gazing on the busy operations of such a school, and watching the multitude of youthful spirits. "They are thus treading in the precincts of an intellectual economy; the economy of thought and truth, in which they are to live forever; and never, to eternity, will they have to regret *this* period and part of their employments. The visitor will be delighted to think how many disciplined actions of the mind, how many just ideas, distinctly admitted, that were strangers at the beginning of the day's exercise,—and among these ideas, some to remind them of God and their highest interest,—there will have been, by the time the busy and well-ordered company breaks up in the evening, and leaves silence within these walls. He will not, indeed, grow romantic in hope; he knows too much of the nature to which these beings belong; knows, therefore, that the desired results of this discipline will but partially follow; but still rejoices to think that partial result, which will most certainly follow, will be worth incomparably more than all it will have cost."

"The friends of these designs for a general and highly-improved education, may proceed further in this course of verifying to themselves the grounds of their assurance of happy results. A number of ideas decidedly the most important that were ever formed in human thought, or imparted from the Supreme Mind, will be so taught in these institutions, that it is absolutely certain they will be fixed irrevocably and forever in the minds of many of the pupils. It will be as impossible to erase these ideas from their memories, as to extinguish the stars. And in the case of many, perhaps the majority, of these youthful beings, advancing into the temptations of life, these grand ideas, thus fixed deep in their souls, will distinctly present themselves to the judgment and conscience an incalculable number of times. What a number, if the sum of all these reminiscences of these ideas, in all the minds now assembled in a numerous school, could be conjectured! But if one in a hundred of these recollections, if one in a thousand, shall have the efficacy that it ought to have, who can compute the amount of the good resulting from the tuition which shall have so enforced and fixed these ideas, that they shall be infallibly thus recollected? And is it altogether out of reason to hope that the desired efficacy will, as often as once in a thousand times, attend the luminous rising again of a solemn idea to the view of the mind? Is still less than *this* to be hoped for our unhappy nature, and that, too, while a beneficent God has the superintendence of it?"*

But if this cannot be expected even under the best of means, what can be anticipated without them? What from a school where religion is disowned, and the Bible rejected? Can the Divine blessing be upon *that?* The same Divine bounty that has given the whole of revelation as belonging to us and to our children forever, has connected the assurance of a beneficent influence and power to accompany the teaching of God's Word, and that it never shall be separated from it. It is conveyed in language like the following:—"This is my covenant with them, saith the Lord; my Spirit that is upon thee, and my words which I have put in thy mouth, shall not depart out of thy mouth, nor out of the mouth of thy seed, nor out of the mouth of thy seed's seed, saith the Lord, from henceforth and forever."†

* Foster on Popular Ignorance, ch. 2.

† Is. lix. 21.

But those who argue for the banishment of the Bible from our schools, would take away this pledge and assurance of a blessing from heaven, and would leave the youthful race of immortal beings, defrauded of their inheritance, their birth-right, not indeed to the uncovenanted mercies of God, but to the power and providence of a system that permits no reference to his mercies, and no knowledge of them. These men would shut up the youthful mind in its pursuit of knowledge, and its disciplinary development, within a narrower way, bounded by high blank walls, over which it is forbidden to look, even were that possible; beyond which, stretches an infinite reach of thought and knowledge, a region of bright celestial light, none of which must be let in upon the secular-beaten lane, which alone the young scholar is commissioned to travel. No teacher must presume to communicate an intimation to his pupils concerning that bright land, nor by any conveyance to let in that celestial radiance, lest sectarianism should rush in with it.

IMPORTANCE OF THE BIBLE

AND OF

Religious Instruction in the Female Schools.

ITS INTERDICTION ODIOUS.

IT is ever to be remembered how large a proportion of the children attending our common schools are girls, and the teachers, females; and how peculiarly appropriate and essential for them, both for instruction and government, the lessons of the Sacred Scriptures. What agency is so powerful for training the sensibilities, for refining the manners, for purifying the heart, for directing and establishing the principles, the feelings, the sentiments, the habits of thought, in that gentle, and yet elevated and impressive character, which we wish to see possessed by every woman, and especially every mother of our Republic? Of all motives, those of religion are best adapted and most effectual in the discipline and government of the schools; but especially are religious sanctions and instructions important in female schools. The idea of educating the female mind of our country, in the proposed exclusion of the Bible and of all religious instruction, is really an insult to the common convictions of humanity in a Christian State.

Just think of the absurdity, the tyranny, of placing the children and their teacher under such a regimen, because of the fear of the charge of sectarianism, that the teacher shall not dare to comment even on the simplest, sweetest, most comprehensive sayings, invitations, parables, or actions, of the Saviour of the world! Think of such an espionage and interdiction, that in a lesson, for example, from the Gospel of John, "I am the resurrection and the life, he that believeth in me, though he were dead, yet shall he live; and whosoever liveth and believeth in me, shall never die," the trembling teacher shall not dare so much as tell the listening girls the duty of trusting in such a Saviour, and loving him, and following his example, and resting on him unto life eternal! Shall not dare impress the sweetest, most common, most essential principles of Christianity upon those tender hearts and awakening consciences, for their guidance, their character, their welfare, in this world and in that which is to come! Think of classes and teachers under this fear, lest some inquisitorial commissioner should enter, and mark this process of celestial light as endangering the entrance of sectarianism, and therefore not to be permitted, out of respect to the conscientious rights of those who require the exclusion of the Bible and of all religious instruction.

And yet, this jealousy, espionage, and trembling fear, is inevitable the moment you admit that the simplest religious instruction is sectarian, and that the government have no right to give religious instruction to the children of the State. But such a rule and such an admission is directly contrary to the principles laid down under sanction of the State itself in the foundation of our common school system; nay, contrary to the very definition of education, as given, again and again, by our governors and legislative bodies. It is a monstrous wrong, an oppression and a fraud incalculable, to confound religion and sectarianism, and to assert that because the latter is forbidden, and most justly forbidden, therefore the former shall not be taught, for fear of opening the door for the latter. What a triumph for the Tempter of mankind, if politicians, at the instigation of those who slander the Bible itself as sectarian, can be authorized to exclude religion from our schools, to banish all the lessons of Christianity from the knowledge and affection of the opening minds of those millions of our children who receive no education whatever but that which the State gives them!

The exclusion of the Bible and of all religious bias would be followed inevitably by a fear and jealousy of all religious teaching, and by-and-bye, when any allusion should be made by the teacher to God, Christ, and religious motives and sanctions, there would be an instinctive repulsion, as if this were trenching on forbidden ground. The threat of banishing the teachers, if they do not banish all religious bias from their instruction, would be more and more frequent, and the common schools would come, by common law of practice and exclusion, to be fearful inquisitorial domiciles of jealousy against Divine truth.

Scarcely anything can be conceived more intolerably odious than such a tyrannical interdiction operating on the mind and conscience of the teacher. And yet, this is the very result to which this extreme dread of sectarianism, and the exclusion of all positive religious influence in consequence of that dread, would soon come, if not prevented; and would no more dare to instruct a youthful pupil as to the character of the Saviour and the duty of faith in him, than under the Austrian despotism a teacher would dare instruct his pupils in the nature of civil and religious liberty, and the rights of man. There, everything is free to be taught *but* freedom; and here, it is proposed that everything shall be free to be taught *but the Bible and religion*; the moment you trench upon the province of religious truth, some political informer shall denounce you as a teacher of sectarianism in the public schools. On that subject of religion you must keep you mouth shut; not one word of instruction must you drop, or the inquisitor shall be upon you. You shall not be permitted even to explain a passage of Scripture. If the Bible is read at all in school, or used as a class-book, not a comment must be made upon its instructions, lest you open the door to the horrid monster of sectarianism.

Now, this is anything but compatible with a *free* school system. Yet this very throttling and suffocation of all religious inquiry and communication is contended for, on the plea that if religion is introduced at all, it opens the door for sectarianism, and none can tell where it would stop. By the very same argument, liberty must be choaked and silenced; for any discussion of the principles of *that*, opens the door to anarchy and rebellion; and so the freedom of the press must be stopped, for otherwise it runs into libels and licentiousness. But the answer in all these cases is just this: that when the offence comes, then it is time enough to stop it, and that you have

no right to prevent liberty itself for the purpose of preventing the abuse of liberty. Let the press go free, and when any man abuses that freedom, bring him up for it, to trial and punishment. And just so, let religion go free in the schools, and wait till some sectarian abuses the privilege, and stop the abuse, but not the privilege. Do not put a ban before hand upon religion and religious instruction, under pretence of preventing sectarianism. For religious instruction is one thing, and a thing entirely proper and necessary for the schools; but sectarianism is another thing, and entirely improper. And it is not true that you cannot have religious influence and instruction without sectarianism. Will any one dare to call our Saviour's parables sectarian? Yet under the rule of exclusion contended for, no teacher in the schools might dare explain the least of those parables, not even so much as to tell an energetic child what is the meaning of the pearl of great price. If anything of that kind comes up, some are ready to say, let the child be referred to its parents or its pastor. But suppose it has neither parents nor pastor; or suppose that the pastor is a priest, who hates the Bible, and the parents keep a grog shop. Where, in that case, shall the child be referred to, for a knowledge of the pearl of great price?

One object of a good education is to make the children inquisitive, and the teachers who know their business, will always encourage the asking of questions, and the utmost kindness and freedom in answering them. What is a school worth, that represses all this freedom instead of stimulating it? But shall there be this freedom only on secular, and never on religious things? Suppose you have a class reading in the New Testament. That sweet and blessed passage happens to be in the reading lesson, Come unto me, all ye that labor and are heavy laden, and I will give you rest. Have you got to stop all your faculties of suggestion, of inquiry, of instruction there, and put a hermetical seal on the minds and lips of your pupils, because it is a religious lesson, and on that there must be no comment? If not, how will you get along? Suppose that you ask, (as a good teacher will certainly encourage the art and habit of questioning,) Has any one any questions on the lesson? and suppose that one bright little boy inquires if that verse means the young as well as the old, or who it is that he must come to, or how he must come? Oh, you say, hush, my boy, there must be nothing of religious instruction here; but you may ask your father and mother when you go home. Father and mother! What if the child comes from the Five Points? And why not also send him to father and mother for the solution of his knots and difficulties in questions of grammar and arithmetic? Perhaps in nine cases out of ten, he might be more likely to obtain *that* knowledge at home, than he would to gain any salutary instructions or ideas on the subject of religion.

The foundation of Normal schools, or institutions of education for teachers, to prepare them for their work, is referred by Lord Brougham to Fellenberg, the philosopher of Hofwyl, of whom he thus speaks:—" This happy idea originated with my old and venerable friend, Emanuel Fellenberg, a name not more known than honored, nor more honored than his virtuous and enlightened efforts in the cause of education and for the happiness of mankind, deserve."

And now let us mark Fellenberg's own expression of his feelings to the lamented President Fisk, speaking on the exclusion of the Bible and religion from a common school system of education. He had received a somewhat exaggerated account of the matter in America, and Dr. Fisk gives the conversation as follows:—"Mr. Fellenberg expressed his very great surprise at the neglect of religious instruction in our schools in America; that the Bible was excluded as a regular text-book; in short, that in the United States, among a religious, a Protestant, an enlightened, a free people, man should be educated so much in view of his physical wants, and his temporal existence, while the moral feelings of the heart, and our religious relations to God and eternity, should be left so much out of our schools. But, he said, the great principles of our religion would come into collision with no man's views who believed in Christianity; and that, at any rate, party views were nothing in comparison with the importance of religious training; and therefore every good man ought to be willing to make some sacrifices of party views for the great benefits of an early religious education."

Nothing could be more just and appropriate than these sentiments. They may be conjoined with Professor Stowe's remarks on the moral training in the common schools of Prussia, from his Report on the course of education in those schools.

"Another striking feature of the system," says he, "is its moral and religious character. Its morality is pure and elevated, its religion entirely removed from the narrowness of sectarian bigotry. What parent is there, loving his children, and wishing to have them respected and happy, who would not desire that they should be educated under such a moral and religious influence? Whether a believer in revelation or not, does he not know that without sound morals there can be no happiness, and that there is no morality like the morality of the New Testament? Does he not know that, without religion, the human heart can never be at rest, and that there is no religion like the religion of the Bible? Every well-informed man knows that, as a general fact, it is impossible to impress the obligations of morality with any efficiency on the heart of a child, or even on that of an adult, without an appeal to some code, which is sustained by the authority of God; and for what code will it be possible to claim this authority, if not for the code of the Bible?"

Professor Stowe's able Report should be studied by those who imagine that religious iustruction must of necessity be sectarian. Few things can be more instructive and impressive than his account of the manner in which religious and moral instruction is communicated in select Bible narratives, in friendly and familiar conversation between the teacher and the class. At a somewhat more advanced age, the whole of the historical part of the Bible is studied thoroughly and systematically, without the least sectarian bias, and without a moment being spent on a single idea that will not be of the highest use to the scholar during all his future life.

NECESSITY OF A

Christian Common School Education

FOR A

LIVING AND PROGRESSIVE CIVILIZATION.

It was a very profound remark of the great German Poet and Historian, Schiller, that "it is not enough that all intellectual improvement deserves our regard only so far as it flows back *upon* the character; it must in a manner proceed *from* the character; *since the way to the head must be opened through the heart.*"

The world, therefore, is wholly wrong in this matter of education, when it administers its own medicaments only, its own elements, its own food, and nothing higher, its own knowledge without the celestial *life* of knowledge. Power it gives, without guidance, without principles. It is just as if the art of ship-building should be conducted without helms, and all ships set afloat to be guided by the winds only. For such are the immortal ships on the sea of human life without the Bible; its knowledge, its principles, ought from the first to be as much a part of the educated, intelligent constitution, as the keel or rudder is part and parcel of a well-built ship. Religious instruction, therefore, and the breath of the sacred Scriptures, ought to be breathed into the child's daily life of knowledge, and not put off to the Sabbath, when your children are addressed from the pulpit, or a small portion of the young are gathered into Sabbath Schools. Above all the elements of knowledge, that of religion is for all. If in their daily schools, children were educated for eternity, as well as time, there would be more good citizens, a deeper piety in life, a more sacred order and heaven-like beauty in the republic, a better understanding of law, a more patient obedience of it. If our education would be one that States can live by, and flourish, it must be ordered in the Scriptures.

Romanism, in its attacks against the Word of God, forms a rallying point for all the infidelity and atheism of a country. Whoever and whatever hates the light of the Bible, will shout encouragement to the sect that dares make a crusade against it. All elements of darkness and of evil will come trooping to its assistance. The time for prayer and vigilance, therefore, against its advances, is now. By-and-bye, the genius of a protective piety that has slumbered, may awake when it is too late to avoid great disaster.

Some errors are so subtle and dangerous in their nature, that if you do not take them in their infancy, but allow them to accumulate, you afterwards dare not approach them. You must have a Safety Lamp, or you cannot securely examine them. If you carry the open torch of Truth, they will explode, like the pestiferous mine-gas, and blow you up. If men do not take care, this will be the case with Romanism in its inveterate and deadly antagonism against the Scriptures; there will be such an accumulation of this despotic element, that loves the darkness and hates the light, that it will be as much as a man's life is worth, even to examine it; it has been so in other countries, and some day, if we let it work successfully against the Bible in our schools, it will make an explosion that will shatter our whole system.

Meanwhile, let us beware of the false confidence, that because in a past generation we *have had* the Bible at the foundation, we can now afford to dispense with it. Let us beware of the delusion that a civilization which began *in* Christianity, can be progressive *without* Christianity, or that a freedom, which was the gift *of* heaven and heavenly truth, can be permanent, separated *from* heaven.

"When in the seventeenth century," says the Chevalier Bunsen, "Europe emerged out of the blood and destruction into which the Pope and the Romish or Romanizing dynasties had plunged it, the world, which had seen its double hope blighted, was almost in despair both of religious and of civil liberty. The eighteenth century, not satisfied with the conventional theodicea of that genius of compromise, Leibnitz, found no universal organ for the philosophy of history, except the French Encyclopedic School; and this school had no regenerating and reconstructive idea, save that of perfectibility and progress. But what is humanity without God? What is natural religion? What is progress without its goal? These philosophers were not without belief in the sublime mission of mankind, but they wanted ethical earnestness as much as real learning and depth of thought. They pointed to civilization as to the goal of the race which mankind had to run. But civilization is an empty word, and may be, as China and Byzantium show, a *caput mortuum* of real life, a mummy dressed up in the semblance of living reality."*

* **Hyppolitus and his Age. Vol. 2, p. 8.**

Argument from the History of Common Schools

AND THE

School Statutes, in New York.

THE whole history of the system of common schools in our country is the history of the efforts of men who desired to place the Bible and religious truth in them, and as the foundation of them. Our towns were little republics with the Bible for their foundation. Our schools were little republics also, with the Bible *there*. The idea of divorcing the Bible from common schools, and common schools from the Bible and its religious instructions, would have been repugnant to the whole feeling, conviction, and determination of their founders. It would have been the wreck of any system of education, to propose that the Scriptures, and all religious bias, should be excluded from them; and it will be so still; the country will not bear it. More and more the affections of the people will be alienated from the common schools, if we take the Bible out from them. Respectable, and religious, and well-informed parents, will cease to send their children to them; and they will become the resort only of the careless, the reckless, the utterly poor and destitute, and of those who never at home receive the light of divine truth or enjoy the fostering and restraining influence of a religious education. And when there comes to be such a division, as come there must, if the Bible and religion be excluded from the schools, then will our common schools go down; the most lavish munificence on the part of the State could not keep them up; the most patronising, or even compulsory legislation would be in vain to support them. They depend upon the affection and respect of the moral, the religious, and the better instructed part of the community; and when that ceases, the schools must go into contempt. The conscience of the church in this country cannot long be blinded or stupefied on this subject; it will awake; but it may awake when it is too late to restore to the Word of God the place which it rightfully claims; and then, conscience itself would destroy the school system.

It claims that place, not only rightfully, and from its very authority as the Word of God, but also historically, by long-established law and custom. And we are now to show, by historical survey, and appeals to the Statute Book, as well as to the habit and usage of the States and towns foremost in the work of education, that the plan of excluding the Bible, and all positive religious instruction and influence, is *a new and modern scheme* concocted for a particular political emergency or purpose; *an innovation*, contrary in every case to the views and principles of the founders of the school system, the convictions of the wisest men in our country, the custom of our towns and villages, and the explicit provisions of our school laws.

The History of the Common School system of the State of New York, is full of instruction and warning. It begins with the first meeting of the State Legislature, after the adoption of the Constitution, when the Governor, George Clinton, introduced the great subject in his speech, as follows:

"Neglect of the education of youth, is one of the evils consequent upon war. Perhaps there is scarce anything more worthy your attention, than the revival and encouragement of seminaries of learning; and nothing by which we can more satisfactorily express our gratitude to the Supreme Being for his past favors, since piety and virtue are generally the offspring of an enlightened understanding."

From 1795 to 1802, various measures were adopted, and revenues appropriated for this object. In 1802 and 1803, Gov. Clinton renewedly and energetically recommended the establishment of Common Schools, putting morals and religion as their foremost objects. "The advantage to morals, religion, liberty, and good government, arising from the general diffusion of knowledge, being universally admitted, permit me to recommend this subject to your deliberate attention."

In 1804, Governor Lewis remarked, with reference to the subject of education, and the establishment of Common Schools, as follows: "In a government resting on public opinion, and deriving its chief support from the affections of the people, RELIGION AND MORALITY cannot be too sedulously INCULCATED. COMMON SCHOOLS, under the guidance of respectable teachers, should be established in every village, and the indigent be educated at the public expense."

In 1810, Governor Tompkins called the attention of the Legislature to the subject, in the following language: "I cannot omit this occasion of inviting your at ention to the means of instruction for the rising generation. To enable them to perceive and duly estimate their rights, TO INCULCATE CORRECT PRINCIPLES, AND HABITS OF MORALITY AND RELIGION, and to render them useful citizens, a competent provision for their education is all essential."

In 1811, Governor Tompkins again called the attention of the Legislature to this subject, and a law was passed for appointing five Commissioners, to report a system for the organization and establishment of Common Schools. The Commissioners were men well fitted for this trust, and proved faithful to it. Their masterly document is quoted at large in the official history of the Common School system, with these remarks: "We cannot deem any apology necessary for the space occupied by these extracts from this admirable report; shadowing forth as it does the great features of that system of public instruction subsequently adopted, and successfully carried into execution; and laying down, in language at once eloquent and impressive, those fundamental principles, upon which alone, any system of popular education, in a republic like ours, must be based."

Report of the Commissioners, and Foundation of the System by the State.

LET us then see what, in the view of the founders of our system, were some of those fundamental principles.

"Perhaps," say they, "there never will be presented to the Legislature a subject of more importance than the establishment of Common Schools. Education, as the means of improving the moral and intellectual faculties, is, under all circumstances, a subject of the most imposing consideration. To rescue man from that State of degradation to which he is doomed, unless redeemed by education; to unfold his physical, intellectual, and moral powers; and to fit him for those high destinies which his Creator has prepared for him, cannot fail to excite the most ardent sensibility of the philosopher and the philanthropist."

"The people must possess both intelligence and virtue; intelligence to perceive what is right, and virtue to do what is right. Our republic, therefore, may justly be said to be founded on the intelligence and virtue of the people. For this reason, it is with much propriety that Montesquieu has said, In a republic, the whole force of education is required."

"The Commissioners think it necessary to present in the strongest point of view, the importance and absolute necessity of education, either as connected with the cause of religion and morality, or with the prosperity and existence of our political institutions. The expedient devised by the Legislature is the establishment of Common Schools; which being spread throughout the State, and aided by its bounty, will bring improvement within the reach and power of the humblest citizen. This appears to be the best plan that can be devised to disseminate RELIGION, MORALITY, AND LEARNING throughout a whole country."

It is clear that in the view of these gentlemen, and of the legislature under whom they acted, religion as well as knowledge was a legitimate subject of teaching and dissemination by the government through the public schools. They did not deem the introduction of religious principles an intrusion on the rights of any conscience.

But still further, speaking of the course of instruction appropriate and essential in common schools, under direction and patronage of the State, the commissioners say, "In these schools should be taught at least those branches of education which are indispensably necessary to every person in his intercourse with the world, and to the performance of his duty as a useful citizen. Reading, writing, arithmetic, and the principles of morality, are essential to every person, however humble his situation in life. Without the first, it is impossible to receive those lessons of morality which are inculcated in the writings of the learned and pious; nor is it possible to become acquainted with our political constitutions and laws; nor to decide those great political questions which ultimately are referred to the intelligence of the people. Writing and arithmetic are indispensable in the management of one's private affairs, and to facilitate one's commerce with the world. Morality and religion are the foundation of all that is truly great and good, and are consequently of primary importance." The writers of this report might be supposed to have come to their task fresh from the perusal of Washington's Farewell Address.

In regard to school-masters, they say, "When we consider the tender age at which children are sent to school; the length of time they pass under the direction of their teachers; when we consider that their little minds are to be diverted from their natural propensities to the artificial acquisition of knowledge; that they are to be prepared for the reception of great moral and religious truths, to be inspired with a love of virtue and detestation of vice; we shall forcibly perceive the absolute necessity of suitable qualifications on the part of the master."

Further still, on the subject of proper books, the commissioners declare, that "much good is to be derived from a judicious selection of books, calculated to enlighten the understanding not only, but to improve the heart. And as it is of incalculable consequence to guard the young and tender mind from receiving fallacious impressions, the commissioners cannot omit mentioning this subject as a part of the weighty trust reposed in them. Connected with the introduction of suitable books, the commissioners take the liberty of suggesting that some observations and advice touching the reading of the BIBLE in the schools might be salutary. In order to render the sacred volume productive of the greatest advantage, it should be held in a very different light from that of a common school book. It should be regarded as a book intended for literary improvement not merely, but as inculcating great and indispensable moral truths also. With these impressions, the commissioners are induced to recommend the practice introduced into the New York Free School, of having select chapters read at the opening of the school in the morning, and the like at the close in the afternoon. This is deemed the best mode of preserving the religious regard which is due to the sacred writings."

What could be better than these principles,

accepted and sanctioned by the State as the foundation of a noble system of Free Common School Education? In closing their remarks, the commissioners affirmed that they "could not conclude their report without expressing once more their deep sense of the momentous subject committed to them. If we regard it as connected with the cause of religion and morality merely, its aspect is awfully solemn. But the other views of it already alluded to are sufficient to excite the keenest solicitude in the legislative body. It is a subject, let it be repeated, intimately connected with the permanent prosperity of our political institutions. The American empire is founded on the virtue and intelligence of the people. . . . And the commissioners cannot but hope that that Being who rules the universe in justice and in mercy, who rewards virtue and punishes vice, will most graciously deign to smile benignly on the humble efforts of a people in a cause purely his own, and that he will manifest this pleasure in the lasting prosperity of our country."

If the names of those commissioners under

whose direction the Croton Reservoir was built, to supply this city with pure water, deserved to be engraved in the massive work, much more do the names of these commissioners, at the foundation of our system of Common Free School Education, with the Bible as its corner stone, deserve a grateful and lasting remembrance. They were Jedediah Peck, John Murray, Jr., Samuel Russell, Roger Skinner, and Samuel Macomb. The leading features of the system by them proposed were adopted and passed into a law by the legislature in 1812.

From that time for many years, up to the administration of Governor De Witt Clinton, the system went on improving, and becoming more and more established in the affections of the people. Governor Clinton, in his first message or speech at the opening of the session of 1822, dwelt upon the condition of public instruction, and remarked that "the first duty of a State is to render its citizens virtuous, by intellectual instruction and moral discipline, by enlightening their minds, purifying their hearts, and teaching them their rights and their obligations." Governor Clinton repeatedly wrote upon this subject, and insisted on the duty of elevating the standard of education, mental and moral. He suggested the system of monitorial schools, and we believe also, schools for the training of teachers.

In 1830, Mr. Flagg, the State Superintendent, observed: "The immense importance of elevating the standard of education in the common schools is strongly enforced by the fact, that to every ten persons receiving instruction in the higher schools, there are at least five hundred dependent upon the common schools for their education." And it may be added, how powerful an argument is this for the necessity of having the Bible and religious instruction in these schools, and the absurdity, or rather impossibility, of referring the children to other schools or places of instruction for the Word of God, if not ten children in a hundred were likely ever to obtain such advantages.

In 1838, the Superintendent for the first time began to confound the question of religious instruction with that of sectarianism.

From Washington downwards, men of all classes had acknowledged the necessity of religion as well as morality and knowledge, nor had there ever been any jealousy against instruction on the subject of religion as sectarian. But the element of Romanism was now beginning to make itself felt. Yet still the Bible was recommended as a class-book, and the Superintendent justly remarked that "there can be no ground to apprehend that the schools will be used for the purpose of favoring any particular sect or tenet, if these sacred writings, which are their own safest interpreters, are read without any other comment, than such as may be necessary to explain and enforce by familiar illustration, the lessons of duty which they teach."

In 1840, the Superintendent, John C. Spencer, remarked, that "no plan of education can now be considered complete, which does not embrace a full development of the intellectual faculties, a systematic and careful discipline of the moral feelings, and a preparation of the pupil for the social and political relations which he is destined to sustain in manhood.

It must be conceded that the standard of common school education in this State falls far short of the attainment of these objects."

Now, it is obvious that a systematic and careful discipline of the moral feelings is not possible, without a religious training of the conscience, and the guidance of the Word of God. If this were excluded from a common school education, it would be found miserably lame and defective. In the "social and political relations," indeed, in every way, the most direct and certain mode of making good citizens is to educate them under the power of religious truth. It is by *celestial* observations only, Mr. Coleridge once beautifully remarked, that terrestrial charts can be constructed. You are sure to make the young man a good citizen if you make him a virtuous man; you are not sure to make him a good citizen, if you merely instruct him in secular knowledge.

Beginning of the War against the Scriptures.

Soon after this period a severe conflict was waged between those who maintained the natural and legal right and moral necessity of the Scriptures in the schools, and those who endeavored, at the instigation of the Roman Catholic party, to exclude them. During the superintendence of the lamented Col. Stone, and of his successor, Dr. Reese, these gentlemen labored to restore the Bible to its just place and authority, and exposed themselves to much political abuse and obloquy for so doing.

Previous to the administration of Col. Stone, laws were passed in 1842 and 1843, containing the section forbidding sectarian teaching and books. Under cover of these laws, the effort was driven on to banish the Bible, as being itself a sectarian book, no statute having then been passed to *prevent* its banishment, because it had never been dreamed that the time would come when such a statute would be necessary; the Scriptures having been read daily in all the public schools for forty years, without complaint or opposition.

Col. Stone "advised, counselled, recommended, and remonstrated, terminating his official labors by invoking the interposition of the Legislature," to protect and preserve the schools from having the Bible turned out of them. It was in answer to his eloquent appeals that an amendment to the School Law was enacted in 1844, *prohibiting the Board of Education from excluding the Holy Scriptures from any school.* Notwithstanding this, the ward officers of different schools still maintained the exclusion, and forbade the teachers the privilege of using the Bible. "Many of the teachers," the Superintendent declared, "were thus intimidated, from an apprehension least they should lose their places, which indeed was intimated in some cases, and distinctly threatened in others. Valuable teachers, in several cases, for reading the Bible in their schools, have been actually either dismissed or compelled to resign." As an illustration of the influences and the men by whom the exclusion of the Bible was accomplished, a written order was produced by the teacher of a school, in one of the wards where the Bible was prohibited, which order was served upon him by the trustees of the school, in the words and manner following:—

"Sir By a *unanimos* vote of the trustees Last Meeting all *Secterian* Books *is Requisted to Bee* Removed from the School as it is *thaught* the *Bibl* one it is *Requisted* to *Bee* Removed."

The Superintendent justly remarked, that "the orthography, capitals, and want of punctuation, as well as the beauties of the sentence, exhibited the lofty qualifications of such trustees of common schools to control the interests of popular education." But if the sacred cause and system of a common school education be thrown into the hands of politicians, to be arranged with reference to votes, to please this or that political party, nothing better can be expected. The history of that period shows the danger and disaster inevitable upon such a course; but the efforts of the Roman Catholics to expel the Bible, divide the schools, and distribute the school funds, signally failed, through the merciful overruling providence of God.*

* A controversy, growing out of the same question, ran on in the public journals between Bishop Hughes and Mr. Hale, the well-known independent Editor of the Journal of Commerce. On Mr. Hale's part, the controversy embodied facts, appeals and arguments, of such energy and power for the people, that we cannot but present one passage, of great pith and point, directly connected with our subject:

"The effort of your priests and yourselves, gentlemen," said Mr. Hale, "to get possession of the money appropriated by the State of New York for the support of the Common Schools, has a singular appearance. Bishop Hughes says, '*We come here, denied of our rights.*' Pray, what are the rights here, of a priest who holds his commission and his place by the will of a foreign hierarch, and upon condition of continued obedience. Such a man cannot, in the nature of the case, become an American. He may swear allegiance, and kiss the Bible and the cross ever so many times—he is a foreigner still. He may have the *privilege* of staying here, and being protected by our laws; but as to *rights* for intermeddling with American affairs, he has none. The amount which Catholics pay towards the school-money is exceedingly small, and all your contributions to the State, in every way, are greatly overbalanced by the donations made back to you by our various public institutions. You are almost all foreigners by birth here, in your first generation; you profess a religion subordinated to a foreign head—a religion against which our ancestors entered their solemn protest—a protest which their sons mean to sustain while they live, and hand down from generation to generation while the country endures. Your priests come here on a "*mission*," as they profess, and here, with some men of intelligence and worth, and an army who can neither read nor write, headed by these priests, you clamor for your rights. With the enjoyment of all the privileges of American institution, of liberty, religion and science, bestowed on your landing in our country, you are still discontented. Pray, by what rule should your rights be determined? Shall it be by the measure which would be meted out under a reverse of circumstances to a like company of American Protestants in a Catholic country? You claim the right especially to interfere with the management of our public schools. Pray, had you any such right in the country of your birth, where your religion adjusted rights, and dealt them out? Before Americans entrust you with the management of their public schools, they would like to see the result of your labors in the same way in Catholic countries. Can you point us to some spot in Italy, Spain, Austria, or any other country under the influence of the Catholic Church, where the earliest care of Popery is to establish common schools, in which all the children shall be taught to read, and write, and cipher? We should like to visit that Catholic country, where, in every neighborhood, the district school-house is the centre of interest, and to see the Catholic children as in neat attire they assemble blithely every morning. Is there any such spot in all the dominions of the Pope? No; common schools are the offspring of Protestantism. We can have them, because we are not under the dominion of the Pope. His letter proves conclusively that *Romanism is the enemy of Common Schools*, and popular education in every form. Americans will not, if they are wise, put an institution which they love so much into the hands of its enemies. The glory of our system is universal education; the glory of yours is universal ignorance. The meridian of Catholic ascendency was the midnight of our world's history. While our children are taught the elements of all sorts of useful knowledge, and each with a Bible in his hand, is instructed to read, and think, and act independently, our institutions will be safe; but such a system will lay Popery in the dust, wherever it prevails. The common people, in all Catholic countries, are ignorant of the rudiments of education. Those who come here can, in general, sign their names only with a mark. The persons who can neither read nor write, whose numbers disfigure the census returns of our towns, are most of them Catholics. Under all these circumstances, gentlemen, your claim that a part of our Public School money should be put into the hands of Catholic priests to manage, strikes us as exhibiting a wonderful degree of assurance.

Your demand upon us for *proof*, has driven us to a more thorough inquiry into your doctrines and practices than we had ever made before. We have been much instructed by the labor. We believe the assertions which we made, with a wider and deeper feeling of disapprobation now, than when we made them. We find in the system a more daring impiety towards God, and a more confident trust in the credulity of men, and less of even speciousness of scriptural support, than we had supposed. The examination has made us feel more thankful to the great men who dared to face your system in its strength, and more thankful to God that he gave success to their efforts, so that the chains of Popery were broken, and a spirit of freedom let loose which has blessed our land, and will bless all the nations.

Your whole system is anti-American. The powers of your ecclesiastical officers are derived from a foreign prince, and dependent on him. Everything concentrates in him as the head of your system. By authority received from him it is that Bishop Dubois shuts up one American church, and maintains a man, publicly charged by numerous affidavits with being often intoxicated, as the priest of another, in defiance of the will of the people. There is no Americanism in this. You, gentlemen, while you own the supremacy of the priests in such a matter, and humbly crouch to their power, are deficient in the first elements of Americans. To be an American, is not to live on American soil only, but it is to be a freeman in politics and religion. It is to be free to read, to think, to act, and to *control* our own affairs.

If, standing as you do, you suppose that by any means you can get possession of our public institutions, especially of our public schools, or any part of them, for the purpose of perverting them from their public, American character, to the sectarian subordination of Romanism, you are mistaken. Do not infer more than is meant from the readiness with which you are admitted to all the benefits of our institutions. Americans have no reason to fear you, and no wish to embarrass you. They trust in Liberty as their shield. They believe that its principles are so thoroughly established and protected by a free press, and all the means of free discussion among the people, that despotism cannot be introduced, either in politics or religion, and made to flourish here.

However enslaved the feelings of persons may be when they come from the despotisms of the old world, and although that slavery may be so inwrought that the subject cannot at once be disenthralled when he treads our shore, they yet believe that our atmosphere of liberty will revive the vitality of manliness within him, and that at least his *children* will be true Americans. We have never thought of subordinating the moral and intellectual machinery which works this renovation, to the control of new and uninstructed hands. Politicians may be supple to you, and if you will offer yourselves for sale for the boon you demand, some of those politicians may be willing to sell their birth-right for your votes. But it is not so with the people. They understand something of the Anti-American character of your system, and they will displace any man who is found betraying the public interest to you. You and all other citizens are at liberty to construct schools as you please, for yourselves. But the public schools must remain public, subordinated to no religious sect, yet unobjectionable to all. They are not designed to teach religion, yet the Bible, the common book of all sects, they retain, and will retain, as God prepared it for man's use, without note or comment of human addition. *The Bible is the corner-stone of our whole fabric, and that book in the vernacular tongue, in the hands of everybody, is the grand principle of Americanism. You must conform to this principle if you would be Americans.* If you find the Bible a sectarian book, favorable to other sects, and dangerous to your's, the reason probably is, that your opinions are less in accordance with the Bible than theirs. Let us invite you therefore, gentlemen, to adopt the American plan of liberty: to discard the timorous fear of error, and trust to the mighty power of truth. Cast off, for yourselves, and your people, the slavery of priests and councils, and invite every man to go to the fountains of truth, and taste and judge for himself. Unite with us in maintaining our public schools and all our other public institutions on a public basis. If your system should be overthrown by the free energies of truth, you will have, as Americans, and as men, as much occasion to rejoice in the triumph, as any of your fellow-citizens, If, on the same free plan, the Roman Catholic religion can supplant Protestantism, so be it, we say, Let truth prevail. It is that alone which can sustain useful institutions in this world, and prepare us for the world of realities to which we hasten."

Establishment of the Free School System.

RENEWAL OF THE WAR AGAINST THE SCRIPTURES.

In 1849, the act was passed establishing free schools throughout the State—our present free school system—determined by popular vote, the whole number of votes cast being 249,872, and the majority in favor of the law, 157,921. On the question for the repeal of this system, there were cast 393,654 votes, 184,398 for the repeal, and 209,346 against it; leaving a majority of 25,038 against repealing it. An annual tax of 800,000 dollars for the support of free schools, is provided for in this system, in addition to which there is a school fund of more than five million and four hundred thousand dollars, so that the whole annual amount applicable to the support of free schools is one million and one hundred thousand dollars. The responsibility devolving upon the State Superintendent at the head of this vast system is immense, and the report of Mr. Morgan in 1851, was an admirable development of the grand and comprehensive character, moral and intellectual, which this system should possess. The history of the system, prepared under his direction, remarks that "there is no institution within the range of civilization, upon which so much for good or for evil depends, upon which hang so many and such important issues to the future well-being of individuals and communities, as the common district school. It is through that alembic that the lessons of the nursery and the family fire-side, the earliest instructions in pure morality, and the precepts and examples of the social circle are distilled; and from it those lessons are destined to assume that tinge and hue which are permanently to be incorporated into the character and the life." The grandest and best results from this school system it is declared can be anticipated, but only "by an infusion into its entire course of discipline and instruction of that *high moral cul-*

ture, which alone can adequately realize the idea of sound education." "The means of elementary instruction demand and will repay the consecration of the highest intellectual and moral energies, the most comprehensive benevolence, and the best affections of our common nature."

From the preceding sketch of this system, taken from the public documents, it will be perceived that while the greatest care has been justly taken to exclude sectarianism, its founders and promoters were equally careful and determined that the Bible and religion should *not* be excluded; they intended and provided that moral and religious instruction should possess a fundamental place and influence. With such a purpose, they commended the enterprise to God, and to the religious convictions of the country.

Accordingly, provision was early made by law, giving opportunity for the exercise of a religious influence by the teachers, yet not sectarian; and under Mr. Spencer's administration it was decided, and the enactment is part of the system, that "Teachers may open and close their schools with prayer, and the reading of the Scriptures, accompanied with suitable remarks, taking care to avoid all discussion of controverted points, or sectarian dogmas."*

And yet, in the face of this decision, and of usage hitherto, it is now directly asserted that to give this permission to the teachers will be to trample upon conscience, and open the door to sectarianism, and take away the rights of those who do not believe in the importance and efficacy of prayer! It is asserted that even though the reading of the Scriptures were permitted, yet, to say one word as to their meaning, to explain, illustrate, or enforce their lessons, is an intrusion on the universal conscience, and especially on the Romish conscience, and ought not to be suffered. And by various influences and edicts, personal and oral, and contrary to the public enactments, the Bible itself has in some cases been excluded, and the endeavor has been made, and in some instances successfully, to introduce a

* Randall's Common School System of the State of New York, p. 273.

secret, silent, inquisitorial common law against all prayer and religious instruction, and to produce the impression that anything bordering on religious truth will endanger the popularity of the teachers and the schools, expose them to the charge of sectarianism, and be regarded with suspicion and disfavor by the appointed school authorities. In some cases the teachers have been publicly threatened that if they do not drop those practices, nay, if they even persist in using the Lord's prayer, they shall be turned out of their places. Such threats have been made to female teachers, even in the presence of the children, and no redress has been granted for the insult.

Whence has sprung so rapid and alarming a change, in subversion or utter disregard and violation, of some of the best and earliest established fixtures of the public school system? Whence has arisen this restraint, this fear, this ban upon the Bible and religion, notwithstanding the known fact that the use of the Bible and religious instruction has been the wont of the schools from the beginning, and to exclude it now, on pretence of its being sectarian, would be a departure from the provision and recommendation of the fathers and framers of the school system, and from the custom and law hitherto?

It is impossible, and perhaps it would be useless, in this place, to go into a history of the introduction of the Romish and political element into the management of a system of public education, that ought to be so high and sacred above all sectarian and political intrigue. We will not enter on the detail of the conflicts fought, the schemes presented, the influences used, the conferences of the school authorities with Bishop Hughes, the submission to his inspection of all the school literature for consideration, the disgraceful blackening of the school books by Romish expurgation, and the partial and temporary giving up of the school system to the dictation of Romish priests. We say partial and temporary; for such things, we trust in God, cannot be repeated; but yet a most disastrous political taint and sectarian influence have been perpetuated; and whereas the most explicit provisions are made in the school laws against sectarianism, its very worst form and power has been admitted, sectarianism against the Word of God itself, and is now playing its game, in some cases encouraged by the very school authorities, who are bound by law to have resisted it.

The prejudice against the Bible and religion, in our schools, on the part of Romanism, has been taken up, and wrought into an argument, and presented and urged in many ways, even with labored ridicule of the use of the Scriptures, and even by the very officers of that school system, the excellence and success of which were declared, by its founders and our fathers, to be indissolubly connected with, and vitally dependent upon, the Bible and religious truth! And the appeal to men's prejudices, and to their dread of ecclesiastical domination, has been artfully made, for the exclusion of the Bible and prayer, on the ground that anything positively religious in the schools would be "the first step, and a decided one, towards placing them under ecclesiastical guardianship and supremacy." And yet this very appeal, with all the sophistry of the demagogue, is made at the instigation of a sect, and for the very purpose of having the conscientious RIGHT of all other sects to the Bible cut down, trampled on, destroyed, at the will of that one despotic sect demanding the exclusion of the Bible, and demanding it on the express grounds of their own ecclesiastical prejudices and canons! And the very first complaint against the Bible has come from that sect, and the very first occasion of the appearance of sectarianism in the schools, from their foundation, has been the intrusion of the sectarianism of that one sect against the Bible. The complaint has never even been made, from any quarter whatever, that sectarian tenets have been taught in any of the schools, but the complaint, the effort, and the enmity, are against the Bible and religion itself in the schools, and men are not found wanting to join with the sect of the Romanists in the sectarian cry.

Now, in point of fact, the perfect freedom of the Bible and its religious lessons, universally, for all, without any distinction of sect whatever, in the schools, is the only complete security for them *against* "ecclesiastical guardianship and supremacy." But the exclusion of the Bible, the imprisonment and excommunication of its lessons, would be the complete and absolute triumph and authority of that form of ecclesiastical guardianship and supremacy, which asserts its superiority to the Bible, and bases its power, its despotism, on the banishment of the Bible from the use and knowledge of the people. And yet, the President of the Board of Education of New York, no longer ago than last August, at a meeting of the American Educational Convention, denounced the reading of the Bible, and all religious instruction, and even the use of the Lord's Prayer, as sectarian, oppressive, and even ridiculous and irrational. He has even asserted that "the State has no means of ascertaining the true religion." "The reading of the Bible in school," said he, "and the repeating of the Lord's Prayer, is ritualistic and not educational. It is not for improvement in secular learning nor in sacred learning." He puts it on the same footing with the reading from the Romish Missal, or the repetition of the name of the Virgin Mary as the Holy Mother of God; and he argues that if we would not be willing to have the latter in the schools, we have no more right to the former, no more right to repeat the Lord's Prayer than the Romish Missal. The statement of such sentiments is enough; they do not need to be refuted. What would Washington have said to such assertions? They cannot but fill every sound and Christian mind with indignation.

But we are compelled to ask, What does this gentleman mean? Is he wholly ignorant of the history and provisions of the school system? And when he avers that religious instruction in the schools would be "the first step towards placing them under ecclesiastical guardianship and supremacy," has he forgotten that the very founders and framers of the school system did themselves, and the legislature at their suggestion, provide a place for such instruction, and for the Bible, in the schools, and so took that first step? Is he ready to denounce such men as Governor Clinton, Governor Lewis, Governor Tompkins, and the illustrious Commissioners, whose Report stands sanctioned by law and public approbation, as religious sectarians, and the authors of a system of "sectarian propagandism"? Would be the first step! And yet, it has been the custom and law in our school system, ever since we came out from the war of the Revolution! And the very first step, and a daring step it is, too, towards an ecclesiastical despotism in our Common Schools, is this curse and excommunication upon the Scriptures and religious instruction, as sectarian, at the outcry of the Priests and politicians of a religious hierarchy. And this is a desperate argument, (if such incongruous and contradictory assertions can be called argument,) presented by the President of the Board of Education in New York, to an American Educational Convention in Pittsburgh! And although the author must be perfectly well aware that never in any case, has any creed been introduced or sanctioned in the public schools, yet he artfully joins the reading of the Bible, and the use of the Lord's Prayer, with the mention of the Catechism, and the repetition of the Apostles' Creed and the Ten Commandments; and as if there could be no such thing as religion in our schools without sectarianism, denounces the whole as offensive, and demands the entire divorce of secular learning from religion, which he argues should be restricted to the Sabbath Schools.

That it may be seen that nothing is exaggerated, we present the following extract from the address by E. C. Benedict, Esq., President of the Board of Education of New York, delivered before the American Educational Convention in Pittsburgh, August 11, 1853. The despotic style in which Mr. Benedict refers to the conscientious "few," who might complain of the exclusion of the Bible, is to be noted. He assumes that the *right* way of education would be to exclude the Bible and religious instruction, and then says, in effect, that if we take that way, we can afford to despise and disregard the complainants against it, *because of their weakness!* Not an intimation is breathed, or hinted at, that those who demand the continuance of the Bible in our public schools, have any conscience, or any rights in the matter; but they can be despised and trampled on, because they are few and weak!

"We can do right—we can do what ought to satisfy all, and the unfounded complaints of a few will be but the expression of their weakness. What should be our rational rule of conduct? Whenever we can find a few children together shall we compel them to lay aside their occupation for the time and read the Bible, or say their prayers, or perform some other religious duty? Will it be sure to make them better? Will it be sure to give them religious instruction—to require it at the dancing-school, the riding-school, the music-school, the visiting-party, and the play-ground—shall studies, and sports, and plays, and prayers, and Bible, and catechism, be all placed on the same level? Shall we insist that secular learning cannot be well taught unless it is mixed with sacred? Shall algebra and geometry be always interspersed with religion instead of *quod erat demonstrandum*. Shall we say *selah* and *amen?* Shall we bow at the sign plus? Can we not learn the multiplication table without saying grace over it? So of religious instruction, will it be improved by a mixture of profane learning? Shall the child be taught to mix his spelling lessons with his prayers, and his table-book with his catechism? If there were any necessary relation between religious and secular instruction, which required that they should be kept together, the subject would have another aspect. But no one has ever maintained that the religious teacher, the minister of religion and the office-bearers in the church, should mix secular instruction with their more solemn and sacred inculcations. I should be almost charged with profanity, if I should attempt to exhibit the sacrilegious folly of mixing these earthly alloys with the precious and virgin gold of divine truth; if I should exhibit the preacher as pointing to the grammatical construction, the rhetorical finish, the oratorical display of his discourses as a necessary part of his teaching in the sacred desk; if I should show you the ritual of the church prescribing mathematics and metaphysics for fast days, and Belle Lettres for festivals, and subjecting the mysterious and life-giving elements of the holy eucharist to the analysis of a chemical lecture. No, no, these sacred matters are set apart; they are themselves alone; they are by divine appointment intrusted to appropriate keeping, and let us beware that we are not struck down, if by extending our profane aid to the ark of God, we doubt the sufficiency of the divine protection.

"Now, the reading of the Bible, the repeating of the Lord's Prayer, the Apostles' Creed, and the Ten Commandments in school, is ritualistic and not educational. It is not for improvement in secular learning, nor in sacred learning. It is intended merely as a religious ceremony, and, if it give offence, is it not an unnecessary offence? What if we say no one has a right to be offended, still we have no right to offend them, and deprive them of an inestimable blessing by mixing with it what to them is not only unpleasant and repulsive, but, in their opinion, unwholesome. Turn the tables—substitute for the reading of the Scriptures at the opening of the schools the simplest and least offensive of the religious ceremonies of the Roman Catholic Church—reading from the missal some portions of it to which in itself there would be no objection; insist that the school shall bow at the name of Jesus; shall always speak of the Virgin Mary as the Blessed Virgin, or the Holy Mother of God, and see if all of us would be willing to send our children there day by day. See if the pulpits and the ecclesiastical conventions throughout the land would not re-echo the word of alarm; and why should we compel the Jews, who are numerous in our cities, to listen to the New Testament; to repeat the Lord's Prayer, or the Apostles' Creed, or be taught the mysteries of redemption, or leave the schools?"

Mr. Benedict speaks of "overthrowing the great question of Common Schools by a mere form or ceremony." What is meant by overthrowing a question, it would be difficult to say; what is meant by the declaration, "That the reading of the Bible is not for improvement, but is a mere ceremony, and a profane aid to the ark of God," may be more clear; and the assertion, "That there is not only no necessary relation between religious and secular instruction, but that the mingling of them is sacrilegious folly," seems an extreme of combined shallowness and hardihood, upon which no man in his senses could have stumbled. Yet here, in this production, it is deliberately presented to a Christian community! Let this address be placed alongside the Report of the State Commissioners above quoted, and the various provisions, recommendations, and laws in the School System, for fifty years; and also let it be compared with the sentiments and recommendations of Washington, Story, Webster, Clinton, Tompkins, Lewis, Chancellor Kent, and other eminent civil as well as religious writers on this subject still living. Especially let us now set it in comparison and contrast with a portion of Mr. Webster's celebrated argument, of such incomparable beauty and power, in regard to the inevitable infidel tendency of any scheme of education that excludes religion, and the necessity of constantly mingling, with all other knowledge, instruction in religious truth.

Argument of Daniel Webster

AGAINST THE PLAN OF EDUCATION WITHOUT THE BIBLE.*

"The children," said Mr. Webster, "are taken before they know the alphabet. They are kept till the period of early manhood, and then sent out into the world to enter upon its business and affairs. By this time the character will have been stamped. For if there is any truth in the Bible, if there is any truth in those oracles which soar above all human authority, or if anything be established as a general fact by the experience of mankind, in this first third of human life the character is formed. And what sort of a character is likely to be made by this process, this experimental system of instruction? What is likely to be the effect of this system on the minds of these children, thus left solely to its pernicious influence, with no one to care for their

* Before the Supreme Court of the United States, in the case of Girard.

spiritual welfare in this world or the next? They are to be left entirely to the tender mercies of those who will try upon them this experiment of moral philosophy or philosophical morality. Morality without sentiment; benevolence towards man, without a sense of responsibility towards God; the duties of this life performed without any reference to the life which is to come; such is this theory of useful education.

"The scheme is derogatory to Christianity, because it rejects Christianity from the education of youth, by rejecting its teachers, by rejecting the ordinary agencies of instilling the Christian religion into the minds of the young. It is derogatory, because there is a positive rejection of Christianity; because it rejects the ordinary means and agencies of Christianity.

"There is nothing original in this plan. It has its origin in a deistical source, but not from the highest school of infidelity. It is all idle, it is a mockery, and an insult to common sense, to maintain that a school for the instruction of youth, from which Christian instruction by Christian teachers is sedulously and vigorously shut out, is not deistical and infidel both in its purpose and in its tendency. I insist, therefore, that this plan of education is, in this respect, derogatory to Christianity, in opposition to it, and calculated either to subvert or to supersede it.

"In the next place, this scheme of education is derogatory to Christianity, because it proceeds upon the presumption that the Christian religion is not the only true foundation, or any necessary foundation of morals. The ground taken is, that religion is not necessary to morality; that benevolence may be insured by habit, and that all the virtues may flourish, and be safely left to the chance of flourishing, without touching the waters of the living spring of religious responsibility. With him who thinks thus, what can be the value of the Christian revelation? So the Christian world has not thought; for by that Christian world, throughout its broadest extent, it has been and is, held as a fundamental truth, that religion is the only solid basis of morals, and that moral instruction, not resting on this basis, is only a building upon sand. And at what age of the

Christian era have those who professed to teach the Christian religion, or to believe in its authority and importance, not insisted on the absolute necessity of inculcating its principles and its precepts upon the minds of the young? In what age, and by what sect, where, when, by whom, has religious truth been excluded from the education of youth? Nowhere; never. Everywhere, and at all times, it has been and is, regarded as essential. It is of the essence, the vitality, of useful instruction."

Mr. Webster then developed the Divine authority and teaching of the Old and New Testaments on this subject, with such dignity, beauty, and deep feeling, that it would be difficult to find, in all the records of forensic eloquence, anything of greater mastery and power. The extracts which we here reprint, need no apology for their length, because they commend themselves to every mind as the most apt and admirable answer that could be made to the sophistry which would represent religion and religious instruction in our common schools, as a sectarian thing.

"My learned friend," said Mr. Webster,

"has referred with propriety to one of the commandments of the Decalogue; but there is another, a first commandment, and that is a precept of religion, and it is in subordination to this that the moral precepts of the Decalogue are proclaimed. This first great commandment teaches man that there is one, and only one, great First Cause, one, and only one, proper object of human worship. This is the great, the ever fresh, the overflowing fountain of all revealed truth; without it, human life is a desert, of no known termination on any side, but shut in on all sides by a dark and impenetrable horizon. Without the light of this truth, man knows nothing of his origin, and nothing of his end. And when the Decalogue was delivered to the Jews, with this great announcement and command at its head, what said the inspired law-giver? that it should be kept from children? that it should be reserved as a communication fit only for mature age? Far, far otherwise. 'And these words, which I command thee this day, shall be in thy heart. AND THOU SHALT TEACH THEM DILIGENTLY UNTO THY CHILDREN; and shalt talk of them when thou sittest in thine house, and when thou walkest by the way, when thou liest down, and when thou risest up.'

"There is an authority still more imposing and awful. When little children were brought into the presence of the Son of God, his disciples proposed to send them away; but he said, Suffer little children to come unto me. Unto *me;* he did not send them first for lessons in morals to the schools of the Pharisees or to the unbelieving Sadducees, nor to read the precepts and lessons *phylacteried* on the garments of the Jewish Priesthood; he said nothing of different creeds or clashing doctrines; but he opened at once to the youthful mind the everlasting fountain of living waters, the only source of eternal truths: Suffer little children to come *unto me.* And that injunction is of perpetual obligation. It addresses itself to day with the same earnestness and the same authority which attended its first utterance to the Christian world. It is of force everywhere, and at all times. It extends to the ends of the earth, it will reach to the end of time, always and everywhere sounding in the ears of men, with an emphasis which no repetition can weaken, and with an authority which nothing can supersede, Suffer little children to come unto me.

"Before man knows his origin and destiny, he knows that he is to die. Then comes that most urgent and solemn demand for light that ever proceeded, or can proceed, from the profound and anxious broodings of the human soul. *If a man die, shall he live again?* And that question, nothing but God, and the religion of God, can solve. Religion does solve it, and teaches every man that he is to live again, and that the duties of this life have reference to the life which is to come. And hence, since the introduction of Christianity, it has been the duty as it has been the effort of the great and good, to sanctify human knowledge, to bring it to the fount, and to baptize learning into Christianity; to gather up all its productions, its earliest and its latest, its blossoms and its fruits, and lay them all upon the altar of religion and virtue."

Mr. Webster then again exposes, as nothing better than infidelity, the pretence that religious instruction is sectarianism, and the policy of banishing it on that ground. He takes up the objection commonly urged by the opponent of religion, as follows:

"There is such a multitude of sects, and such diversity of opinion, that he will exclude all religion! That is the objection urged by all the lower and more vulgar schools of infidelity throughout the world. In all these schools, called schools of Rationalism in Germany, Socialism in England, and by various other names in various countries which they infest, this is the universal cant. The first step of all these philosophical moralists and regenerators of the human race is to attack the agency through which religion and Christianity are administered to man. But in this there is nothing new or original. We find the same mode of attack and remark in Paine's Age of Reason.

"But this objection to the multitude and differences of sects is but the old story, the old infidel argument. It is notorious that there are certain great religious truths which are admitted and believed by all Christians. All believe in the existence of a God. All believe in the immortality of the soul. All believe in the responsibility, in another world, for our conduct in this. All believe in the divine authority of the New Testament. And cannot all these great truths be taught to children, without their minds being perplexed with clashing doctrines and sectarian controversies? Most certainly they can."

Mr. Webster then takes the supposition of a youth educated, say from six to eighteen, in secular learning merely, without religious teaching, which is the very proposition offered to a Christian community, in the demand that from our common schools the Bible and all religious instruction shall be banished, and carries such a youth into the business of life, and shows what would be the consequence of such a scheme, in the subversion of all morality, Christianity, and government.

"The Christian religion, its general principles, must ever be regarded among us as the foundation of civil society. But this system, in its tendencies and effects, is opposed to all religions of every kind. Religious tenets, I take it, and I suppose it will be generally conceded, mean religious opinions; and if a youth has arrived at the age of eighteen, and has no religious tenets, it is very plain that he has no religion. We will suppose the case of a youth of eighteen, who has just left school, and has gone through an education of philosophical morality. He comes then into the world to choose his religious tenets. The next day, perhaps, after leaving school, he comes into a court of law, to give testimony as a witness. Sir, I protest that by such a system he would be disfranchised. He is asked, 'What is your religion?' His reply is, 'O, I have not yet chosen any; I am going to look round, and see which suits me best.' He is asked, 'Are you a Christian?' He replies, 'That involves religious tenets, and as yet I have not been allowed to entertain any.' Again, 'Do you believe in a future state of rewards and punishments?' And he answers, 'That involves sectarian controversies, which have carefully been kept from me.' 'Do you believe in the existence of a God.' He answers that there are clashing doctrines involved in these things, which he has been taught to have nothing to do with; that the belief in the existence of a God, being one of the first questions of religion, he is shortly about to think of that proposition. Why, sir, it is vain to talk about the destructive tendency of such a system; to argue upon it, is to insult the understanding of every man; *it is mere, sheer, low, ribald, vulgar deism and infidelity!* It opposes all that is in heaven, and all on earth that is worth being on earth. It destroys the connecting link between the creature and the Creator; it opposes that great system of universal benevolence and goodness that binds man to his Maker.

"*No religion till he is eighteen!* What would be the condition of all our families, of all our children, if religious fathers and religious mothers were to teach their sons and daughters no religious tenets till they were eighteen? What would become of their morals, their character, their purity of heart and life, their hope for time and eternity? What would become of all those thousand ties of sweetness, benevolence, love, and Christian feeling, that now render our young men and young maidens like comely plants growing up by a streamlet-side; the graces and the grace of opening manhood, of blossoming womanhood? What would become of all that now renders the social circle lovely and beloved? What would become of society itself? How could it exist? And is that to be considered a charity which strikes at the root of all this; which subverts all the excellence and the charms of social life; which tends to destroy the very foundation and frame-work of society, both in its practices and in its opinions; which subverts the whole decency, the whole morality, as well as the whole Christianity and government of society? No, sir! no, sir!

"It has been said, on the other side, that there was no teaching *against* religion or Christianity in this system. I deny it. The whole is one bold proclamation against Christianity and religion of every creed. The children are to learn to be suspicious of Christianity and religion; to keep clear of it, that their youthful hearts may not become susceptible of the influences of Christianity or religion in the slightest degree. They are to be told and taught that religion is not a matter for the heart or conscience, but for the decision of the cool judgment of maturer years; that at that period when the whole Christian world deem it most desirable to instil the chastening influences of Christianity into the tender and comparatively pure mind and heart of the child, ere the cares and corruptions of the world have reached and seared it, at that period the child is to be carefully excluded therefrom, and to be told that its influence is pernicious and dangerous in the extreme. Why, the whole system is a constant preaching against Christianity and against religion, and I insist that there is no charity, and can be no charity, in that system of instruction from which Christianity is excluded."

And now we ask, in connection with this review of our history in the matter of a common school education, Who have the right to judge and to have their judgment respected, as to the nature of the school system that we need, if not those men of sagacity, patriotism, piety, and comprehensive statesmanship, who founded it for America, for our own country, in view of our own peculiar responsibilities?

The men who founded it for America, and not for Rome; for the wants of our own country, and of those whose whole dependence is on God and the truth, and freedom of the truth everywhere, and not for those who depend upon the darkness, nor with reference to that system which can flourish only in exclusion of the light. It is an American system, not Austrian, nor Roman, nor European, that we are to support, and therefore an education under Divine Truth is needed. A merely secular education may be sufficient in Europe, where governments rule by bayonets, but not here, where government depends on the intelligence, morality, and religion of the people. Where another nation might flourish upon mere secularism, we should go down. We cannot divorce education from religion, and sustain the Republic.

A deliberate argument for the divorce of education from religion is so astounding an occurrence among a Christian people, that we do not wonder that those abroad, in whose way such an argument may have happened to fall, should assert, as they have done, that the element of religion is absolutely not introducable into our educational system, on account of peculiarities in our habits, and in the theory and practice of our national and State governments. And then they base upon this prodigious misconception or falsehood, their conclusion, that after all, the exclusion of religion from a system of public education cannot be so very dreadful or dangerous a thing, if in a country like the United States the people can grow up without it, so religious and so prosperous.

Now, even our limited historical surveys will have shown that our educational system, so far from excluding religious principle, religious instruction, and a religious bias, has been for a longer time and to a greater extent, based upon the Bible, and carried forward with religious truth as its vital element, than any other educational system in the world. Our religion and prosperity as a people are owing to this reality, this religious educational training, and have *not* been gained or maintained in the neglect or exclusion of religious truth. The rejection of the Bible and of all religious bias, from our. systems of education, wherever attempted, or partially successful, is an innovation; a very daring and dangerous innovation, for the most part attempted and accomplished at the instigation of political demagogues, catering for Romish votes. We wish the people of England to understand this. We wish them to understand that till within a very few years the Bible and religion have been free in all our schools, and are so still by law, and in most places by custom; and that it is only by infidel, Romish, and political intrigue and management, that anywhere religious truth is shut out.

Singular Example of Sectarian Legislation against the Christian Sabbath.

In their eager zeal against sectarianism, the history of the school system shows that our school authorities and legislators have sometimes run into the very evil they were so anxious to avoid. This is painfully manifest in a decision incorporated into the body of School Laws, and published in chapter VIII., having therefore the sanction of the State; a decision disposing of the Christian Sabbath as follows:—"Schools may be kept on Sunday for the benefit of those persons who observe Saturday as holy time, and the teacher must be paid for that day by those who send to School."

The inconsiderateness and impropriety of this legislation, and its inconsistency with all the provisions of the school laws against sectarianism, will appear manifest on a moment's consideration.

Indeed, if ever there was sectarian legislation, this is such. It singles out the Jews, and legislates in their behalf, constituting in reality for them a sectional and sectarian school, on the very ground of their sectarianism, and because of it. It takes them into a peculiar union with the State, and that, too, in defiance of the conscientious scruples of nearly all other denominations united. It is not only a profanation of the Christian Sabbath by law, but it goes the whole length of declaring that the Christian Sabbath has no divine sanction, is not a divinely-appointed day to be kept holy, but may properly be spent in a secular employment. It singles out the Jewish Sabbath as more holy than the Christian Sabbath, because it is a distinct provision for the profanation of the Christian Sabbath, by an employment for which the Jewish Sabbath is considered as *too* holy. It is not satisfied with leaving the Jews at liberty to do what they please, either on their Sabbath, or the Christian Sabbath, but it takes hold with them, and makes itself part and parcel with them, in their profanation of the Christian Sabbath. It gives them the advantage of the free common school system, for the profanation of the Lord's Day, by the same employment which they would consider a profanation of the Jewish Sabbath, but which, by a legislation in behalf of their particular conscience, is declared to be no profanation of the Christian Sabbath.

An institution, supported by the people, is used in this case for the profanation of the Christian Sabbath. If it were *no* profanation to keep the common schools on holy time, then no reason why the Jews should not, as all the others, use the *Saturday* for that purpose, and no need of any law for them, permitting them to take the *Christian Sabbath*; but if it *were* a profanation to keep the common schools on holy time, then *as much* a profanation of the Christian as of the Jewish; but the State, in making this law, does really declare that it is a profanation of the *Jewish*, but no profanation of the *Christian*. The

State deliberately chooses the conscience of the Jew, and allies itself with that, in preference to the conscience of the Christian, and our institution, which Christians are taxed to support, is, by law, applied to enable the Jews to profane the Christian's holy day. This is verily an outrage, not only on Christianity, but upon the conscientious rights of the Christian. The State is not content with leaving Jews and Christians to do as they please on their respective Sabbaths, the Jews having the right of teaching their children or not, and the Christians the right of teaching their's or not; but it compels the Christians to sustain and sanction the Jews, in the work of profaning the Christian Sabbath. It takes the school-houses of the people, and applies them to that purpose, and it takes the money of the people to support those schools.

But this is not all. There must be teachers on Sunday, and for all branches taught on any day of the week, and if a corps of Jewish teachers be marshalled and appointed for that day, this makes a double sectarianism adopted by the State. But if not the Jewish teachers, and others should refuse, then might you see the anomaly of the ordinary Christian teachers of our common schools dismissed from their employment, for refusing to serve the Jews on the Christian Sabbath. There is no alternative, if this provision be carried out. Either Jewish teachers must be hired for that particular day, under the authority and care of the State, or the ordinary teachers must continue their services, and so be deprived of their Sabbath, and made to labor in their employment incessantly, seven days in the week. Some persons must do the teaching thus provided for, thus authorized by the State on the Christian Sabbath. Shall it be Jewish teachers, employed because of their sectarianism, and with direct reference to that? This makes a sectarian school. Shall it be other teachers, compelled or hired to continue their ordinary week-teaching through the Christian Sabbath, for the accommodation of Jewish prejudices? This makes it doubly sectarian and oppressive.

Now, if any superintendent, or any member of the legislature, had proposed a bill for the establishment of a Sabbath School, technically so-called, that is, a school for doctrinal religious instruction, in connection with, and as part of the common school system, a school for children in religion on the Sabbath, in the public school rooms, to be used for that purpose, undoubtedly there would have been a great cry made against *this* measure, as *sectarian.* But provision under law cannot only be proposed, but established for the *profanation* of the Christian Sabbath by *secular* instruction *as on all other days*, for the convenience and accommodation of the Jews, or other like sects, and *that* measure is not regarded as sectarian, or partial, or improper! Could there be a more glaring anomaly and inconsistency? The eager desire to be extremely liberal, and to have the school system removed to the farthest opposite point from the iniquity of sectarianism, has caused our legislators or Superintendents to over-vault themselves, and fall on the other side. The effort to make the system of education a political stalking-horse, produced the same result, when the school-books were mangled and mutilated at the command of the sect of Romanists. But this intrusion on the Sabbath is worse in some respects than that sectarian foray upon the school-books. It is a deliberate legalized profanation of the Lord's Day.

But some will answer, Do you call instructing the poor, or the rich, or any children, in reading, writing, and arithmetic on the Sabbath, a profanation of the Sabbath? Nay, not we have done this, but the State. The appointed School authorities take the opinion and conscience of the Jews, that such employment, such secular instruction, *is* a *profanation of holy time*, and by law protect that conscience, and provide for their profaning the holy time of the *Christian* Sabbath instead of the Jewish, by precisely the same employment. If it be a profanation of the Jews' Sabbath, on the plea that *that* is holy time, it is just as much a profanation of the Christian Sabbath, if *that* is holy time. The State authorities have declared that it *is* a profanation of the *Jews'* Sabbath, and *on that account* have given them the *Christian* Sabbath to profane instead.

If it is a profanation of the Jews' Sabbath, then also a profanation of the Christian; but if *not* a profanation of the Jews' Sabbath, then no need of giving them the Christian Sabbath for such profanation instead of their own. But by this peculiar legislation the State has in effect declared that common school instruction is a profanation of holy time, and therefore a profanation of the Christian Sabbath, if *that* be holy time. But the Christian religion establishes it as holy time, as unquestionably as the Jewish religion establishes the Jewish Sabbath as holy time; and therefore the legislature, (for it is under their sanction that this law is engrossed and published,) in ordaining that the Christian Sabbath shall be given up to the Jews for common school instruction, instead of the Jewish Sabbath, have elected and inaugurated the Jewish religion as more sacred than the Christian. And yet, they seem not to have dreamed of there being anything sectarian in such Jewish and unchristian legislation.

The dilemma is as follows: We take first the supposition that the legislature believe in a Sabbath. Then it follows that the legislature either believe the *Christian* Sabbath to be *holy time* or not. If not, (if the character of such sacredness do not belong to the idea and nature of the Sabbath,) then neither is the *Jewish* Sabbath holy time; so that the instruction of the Jews might as well go on upon that day, as any other. But if it *be* holy time, then common school instruction of the Jews is a profanation of the Christian, as well as of the Jews' Sabbath.

But again, on the supposition that such sacredness *does* belong to the nature of the true Sabbath, either the legislature believe that the *Jews'* Sabbath is holy time, or not. If not, then the Christian Sabbath *is;* and they have no right to provide for the violation of the Christian Sabbath by those who disregard it. Disregard it they may, for themselves, but the legislature have no right to provide for such disregard by law.

On the other hand, if they believe the *Jewish* Sabbath to be holy time, the true Sabbath, then they have no right, in direct contravention of that belief, to profane that day, Saturday, by the secular instruction of any of the children in any of the schools. They should shut the schools, and keep the holy time holy, after the example of the Jews; unless, indeed, they will institute *Sabbath* schools of a Saturday, which again would be violently opposed as sectarian.

But once more. The legislature and the people either believe one day or the other, to be holy time, or neither. If neither be holy time, then they have no right to legislate for the keeping of either in preference to the other.

But here, perhaps, some one is ready to say that the legislature, or the superintendents under sanction of the legislature, though believing or admitting that Sunday is the Christian Sabbath, yet legislated for its profanation to ease the conscience of the Jews, and supply their loss of Saturday by a sacrifice to them of our Sunday. But this, again, is just robbing Peter to pay Paul. Or rather, it is robbing God, to make way for human opinion and convenience. It is the scene of Christian legislators violating their own consciences, and the conscience of all the people who believe in the holiness of the Christian Sabbath, to enable the Jews to pursue their worldly avocations on the Lord's Day. If the case were, to enable the Jews to avoid violating their conscience in profaning their Sabbath, it would be quite different. But there is no compulsion either way. If there were, and one party or the other were under necessity of such profanation, the question then might be, whether the legislature and all Christian sects should violate *their* conscience for the ease of the Jews, or the Jews *their's* for the ease of all the rest.

But that is not the case, and cannot be. No Jew, nor any person that keeps Saturday as holy time, is compelled to violate it; and, at the uttermost, in the case before us, the cost of keeping it can be only the loss of a half-day's secular instruction, since none of the schools are kept more than half the day on Saturday. But, on the contrary, it is the case of a Christian legislature giving up the *whole* Christian Sabbath for profanation, in order to supply the loss of half the Jewish Sabbath, considered too sacred to *be* profaned. The idea and acknowledgement of *profanation* lies inevitably embraced in the very exemption of the Jews from secular instruction in *holy time*, and their compensation by giving them the Christian Sabbath instead of their own for such acknowledged profanation. The bare insertion of the condition that those who send that day shall pay the teacher, makes little difference, since the school-houses, and the whole prerogative, provision, and advantage of the system, are bestowed for their use.

Common School System of Connecticut.

THE historical example of Connecticut is interesting and instructive. As early as 1656, explicit laws were added to the general law by which the schools were first instituted, and the deputies, constables, and other officers in public trust, were required to take care "that all their children and apprentices as they grow capable, may, through God's blessing, attain at least so much as to be able duly to read the Scriptures, and other good and profitable printed books in the English tongue, and in some competent measure to understand the main grounds and principles of the Christian religion necessary to salvation." By repeated legislation, and patient effort, the school system was brought to such a degree of efficacy, that, as President Kingsley remarked, "for nearly a century and a half, a native of Connecticut, of mature age, unable to read the English tongue, has been looked upon as a prodigy. The source of the wide-spread and incalculable benefit of popular education in America," President Kingsley continues, "may be traced, without danger of error, to a few of the leading Puritans. If the early Pilgrims, more particularly of Massachusetts and Connecticut, had not struggled and toiled for this great object, and if they had not been immediately succeeded by men who had imbibed a large portion of the same spirit, the school-system of New England would not now exist."

"The schools of this State," says the Connecticut Common School Journal, "were founded and supported chiefly for the purpose of perpetuating civil and religious knowledge and liberty, as the early laws of the colony explicitly declare. Those laws, some of which were published in the first number of this Journal, as clearly declare, that the chief means to be used to attain those objects, was the reading of the Holy Scriptures.

"In many schools, in later years, the Bible has not been used; though there is reason to believe that the ancient custom of our venerable ancestors has recently been gradually reviving. Circumstances have favored its restoration; and increasing light on the principles of sound education cannot fail to establish it everywhere.

"Certificates are in our hands, from experienced instructors out of this State, which bear strong testimony to the happy influences exerted in their schools, by the daily use of the Scriptures.

"Different teachers we have seen, who used the Bible in different ways: some as a class-book, some as a text-book; and it is interesting to see in how many forms it may be brought into use. Some teachers, with a map of Palestine before them, will give most interesting lessons on almost any book in the Bible, by mingling geography, history, ancient manners and customs, with moral and religious considerations. Others make the Bible the law-book of the school; and by showing that they consider themselves and their pupils equally bound to conform their lives and thoughts to its sacred dictates, exercise a species of discipline of the happiest kind. Others still, by the aid of printed questions, or some systematic plan of study, employ the Bible in training the intellect, storing the memory, and furnishing the fancy with the richest treasures of literature. Others think that the various styles found in the sacred volume, offer the very best exercises for practice in reading with propriety and effect; while a critical attention to the character, situation, and feelings of the speakers, which such exercises require, has favorable moral influences. Finally, other teachers believe that the daily reading of the Bible in schools, is of essential benefit to the pupils in various ways; and that the frequent repetition of the Word of God in the hearing even of those too young to read, is an inestimable blessing—a part of the birthright of every child in a Christian land, which cannot be rightfully withholden.

"To these views our readers may add their own as they often and seriously consider the subject. It is one which will probably be ever esteemed a vital one in Connecticut; and if Monsieur Cousin so warmly urged upon the government of France, to make religious instruction the corner-stone of their national system of education, and urged with success the example of Prussia, we may with greater confidence invite the people of our State to supply their schools with the Scriptures, and point to the laws passed by their fathers for this very end, nearly two centuries ago, and (so far as we have the ability to comprehend so vast a subject) to the noble effects produced even by their imperfect observance."

"The interests of education," says Chancellor Kent, speaking particularly of the State of Connecticut, "had engaged the attention of the New England colonists from the earliest settlement of the country; and the system of common and grammar schools and of academical and collegiate instruction, was interwoven with the primitive views and institutions of the Puritans. Everything in their genius and disposition was favorable to the growth of freedom and learning, but with a tendency to stern regulations for the maintenance of civil and religious order. They were a grave and thinking people, of much energy of character, and of lofty and determined purpose. Religion was with them a deep and powerful sentiment, and of absorbing interest. The first emigrants had studied the oracles of truth as a text-book, and they were profoundly affected by the unqualified commands, the awful sanctions, and the sublime views and animating hopes and consolations which accompanied the revelation of life and immortality. . . . . . . The avowed object of their emigration to New England was to enjoy and propagate the reformed Protestant faith in the purity of its discipline and worship. They intended to found republics on the basis of Christianity, and to secure religious liberty under the auspices of a commonwealth. With this primary view they were early led to make strict provision for common school education, and the religious instruction of the people. . . . . The Word of God was at that time almost the sole object of their solicitude and studies, and the principal design in planting themselves on the banks of the Connecticut was to preserve the liberty and purity of the gospel. . . . . We meet with the system of common schools in the earliest of the colonial records. Strict and accurate provision was made by law for the support of schools in each town, and a grammar school in each county; and even family instruction was placed under the vigilant supervision of the selectmen of the town. This system of free schools, sustained and enforced by law, has been attended with momentous results, and it has communicated to the people of this State, and to every other part of New England in which the system has prevailed, the blessings of order and security to an extent never before surpassed in the annals of mankind."

Common School System of Massachusetts.

As early as 1647, less than twenty years from the date of their first charter, the Colony of Massachusetts Bay made provision by law for the support of schools at the public expense, for instruction in reading and writing, in every town containing fifty families; and for the support of a grammar-school, the instructor of which should be competent to prepare young men for the University, in every town containing one hundred families. This was a noble foundation, and it was the religious foresight of the Colonists that laid it. The preamble to the school law runs thus:—"It being one chief object of Satan to keep men from the knowledge of the Scripture, as in former times keeping them in unknown tongues, so in these latter times by persuading them from the use of tongues, that so at least the true sense and meaning of the original might be clouded and corrupted with false glosses of deceivers, therefore to the end that learning may not be buried in the graves of our forefathers in church and commonwealth, the Lord assisting our endeavors, it is ordered by this Court, and the authority thereof, that every township," &c.

By this school law, provision was not only made for the schools, but for the religious character of the teachers, and none others but persons of religious faith and life were admitted, or suffered "to be continued in the office or place of teaching, educating, or instructing youth or children in college or schools."

"Whatever were the causes," says Mr. Carter in his letters to Wm. Prescott, "which led the Puritans of New England to the adoption of their liberal and enlightened policy in regard to free schools, the effects were certainly most happy upon the condition of the people. And with the advantages of their experience, and of living in a more enlightened age, we could hardly hope, on the whole, to make more noble exertions for the promotion of the same object. Their pious care of the morals of the young; their deep and devoted interest in the general dissemination of knowledge; and the sacrifices they endured to afford encouragement and patronage to those nurseries of piety and knowledge, the free schools, are without parallel in the history of this or any other country."

Nurseries of piety and knowledge, because the Bible and its religious instruction were their foundation, and the children in them were trained under religious motives. But our forefathers would have rejected with horror the thought of excluding the Bible and religious instruction from the schools.

The school laws of Massachusetts contain the following comprehensive, religious, and remarkable enactment:—

"It shall be the duty of the president, professors, and tutors of the University at Cambridge, and of the several colleges, and of all preceptors and teachers of academies, and all other instructors of youth, to exert their best endeavors to impress on the minds of children and youth, committed to their care and instruction, the principles of piety, justice, and a sacred regard to truth, love to their country, humanity, and universal benevolence, sobriety, industry, and frugality, chastity, moderation, and temperance, and those other virtues which are the ornament of human society and the basis upon which a republican constitution is founded ; and it shall be the duty of such instructors to endeavor to lead their pupils into a clear understanding of the tendency of the above-mentioned virtues, to preserve and perfect a republican constitution, and secure the blessings of liberty, as well as to promote their future happiness; and, also, to point out to them the evil tendency of the opposite vices."

There is no sectarianism in this enactment, but there *is* religion, and a provision for religious instruction. The observance of this one law would, by the blessing of God, produce, as the result of a common school education, an elevated Christian character in every pupil. The inculcation of religious truth is not left to the varying opinions or will of successive school administrations, but is forever binding. No political manager, at the instigation of Romanism, may brand such instruction as sectarian, or accuse the Government of overstepping its functions in teaching the principles of PIETY, and leading the pupils into a clear understanding of them, which yet cannot possibly be done, without the Word of God. The principles of piety cannot possibly be taught in any school, or by any instructor, without religious truth, and a religious bias given to the instruction; so that the theory that no system of public education can be impartial, unless it excludes all distinctive religious teaching, receives here the best possible practical refutation, in the freest and most impartial and unsectarian school-system in the world. But the Bible itself is distinctive religious teaching, and a clear understanding of piety and virtue is not possible without the Bible; if virtue be essential to be taught, the Bible is essential to be taught.

Board of National Popular Education.

In the sixth article of the Constitution of the Board of National Popular Education, there is required from all the teachers "the daily use of the Bible in their several schools, as the basis of that sound Christian education, to the support and extension of which the Board is solemnly pledged." From the Fifth Annual Report of this Board, we select the following paragraphs from a speech by Mr. Sawtell, at the Anniversary in Cleveland, in 1852. We make this quotation, because it presents, by so happy and powerful an illustration, the necessity of a free and open Bible in our common schools, as the only possible way in which our nation can continue self-governed. The Bible for the masses, Mr. Sawtell truly proclaims, is God's great instrument for governing men and nations. The Bible for the millions of the young.

"There is but one alternative. God will have men and nations governed; and they must be governed by one of the two instruments—AN OPEN BIBLE, with its hallowed influences, or A STANDING ARMY WITH BRISTLING BAYONETS. One is the product of God's wisdom, the other, of man's folly; and that nation or people that dare discard, or will not yield to the moral power of the one, must submit to the brute force of the other. Herein do we discover the secret of our ability to govern ourselves. Just so long, and no longer, than we preserve the open Bible in our schools, shall we be capable of self-government. Let me illustrate my meaning by a single fact: During a seven years' residence in France, party politics often ran high in my native land. The whole country, on the eve of a presidential election, seemed like 'Ocean into tempest wrought.' Political editors seemed to be at swords' points; and, to the Frenchman, our ship of State appeared literally to be beating upon the shoals and quicksands of a lee shore; and their cry was, 'She must go down—she can never out-ride the storm.' But the next arrival, perhaps, announced the result of the contest, the triumph and the defeat. The storm had died away—scarcely a ripple to be seen upon the mighty ocean of agitated mind. The farmer had returned quietly to his plough—the mechanic to his shop—the merchant to his counting-house; and those editors, who, to the Frenchman, seemed so belligerent, were playing off their jokes upon each other, as though nothing had happened. And now, the noble ship once more rights herself, obeys her helm, and, with all her canvas spread to the wind, her banners unfurled, her stars and stripes waving at mast-head, she booms onward with accelerated speed and power, to the chagrin and amazement of every despotic power in the Old World; while the Frenchman, with a shrug of the shoulder, would press my hand and exclaim—'You, Americans, are the queerest people in the world. How is it, that you can create such a storm, and your political editors can talk so rabidly, and lash the whole nation, like an ocean, into mountain waves, and yet, the moment the election is over, all is quiet, all seem satisfied? Can you explain it? Why, if such a storm had been raised here in France, blood would have flown to the horse's bridles. Do tell me the secret of that power that can control the multitude, under such excitement?' Well, how did I explain it? I'll tell you in few words:—

"Opening the Bible, I said to the Frenchman—'From this despised and proscribed book, which God has given to illumine the path of every man, emanate the light and the power that control the American mind in such emergencies. Tens of thousands of our citizens who deposit their votes in the ballot box, have been blessed with pious mothers, who brought their infant minds early in contact with God's precious truth. They taught them to commit to memory such passages as these—"He that is slow to anger is better than the mighty, and he that ruleth his spirit, than he that taketh a city." "The fear of the Lord is the beginning of wisdom." "Remember now thy Creator in the days of thy youth."

"Do unto others as ye would that they should do unto you," &c., &c. These and kindred texts were taught them in the nursery, the sabbath school, public schools, by mothers and teachers, as God commands, "when they went out and when they came in, when they sat down and when they rose up," giving them "line upon line, precept upon precept, here a little and there a little," thus engraving them deeply upon the tablets of their hearts, imbuing their infant spirits with the spirit of the gospel—which is "peace on earth and good will to man." Thus they grew up and matured into manhood, with this leaven working in them, both to will and to do that which is just and equal toward God and toward men; and though multitudes there may be, who have not been blessed with this early religious training from an open Bible, yet a sufficient number have been thus trained to exert an all-pervading, controlling influence over the masses; and hence our indebtedness to an OPEN BIBLE, for our ability to govern ourselves. Take from us the open Bible, and like Sampson shorn of his locks, we should become as weak as any other people. Take away the Bible, and like Italy, Austria and Russia, we would need a despot on a throne, and a standing army of half a million, to keep the populace in subjection.' "

With the Bible, men can govern themselves, and despots are superfluous; without the Bible, they are a natural product and necessity of society. Hence the malignant instinct of priestly and monarchical despotism against the Word of God; what have we to do with thee? art thou come hither to torment us before the time? Nothing would more surely lengthen out the lease and life of despotism, than a scheme for the education of children, which should sedulously exclude all Biblical or Christian instruction. Mr. Webster cites a law case, decided in England, in 1842, in the following summary: "Courts of equity, in this country, will not sanction any system of education, in which religion is not included." The freedom and good government of a country are then and there only practically secured, where all the children are educated in the knowledge of the Scriptures.

Custom and Opinion in Massachusetts.

THE common law and opinion in Massachusetts, as well as the statute, protect the right of the Bible and of religious instruction in common schools. It is to be hoped that the effort of the Romanists against the Bible cannot there be successful, though the disastrous experiment of its banishment may be tried in some cases for a season. But if once expelled, its restoration is well-nigh hopeless. *Obsta principiis.* It was Mr. Choate who exclaimed, in one of his orations: "Banish the Bible from our public schools? Never! so long as a piece of Plymouth Rock remains big enough to make a gun-flint out of!" This is the feeling of true patriotism, for our liberty rests upon the instruction of our children in

Divine truth, and "he is the freeman whom the truth makes free."

"So pervading and enduring is the effect of education upon the youthful soul," says Horace Mann, speaking of a common school education, "that it may well be compared to a certain species of writing ink, whose color at first is scarcely perceptible, but which penetrates deeper and grows blacker by age, until, if you consume the scroll over a coal-fire, the characters will still be legible in the cinders. Hence I have always admired that law of the Icelanders, by which, when a minor child commits an offence, the courts first make judicial inquiry whether his parents have given him a good education; and if it be proved they have not, the child is acquitted and the parents are punished. In both the old colonies of Plymouth and of Massachusetts Bay, if a child over sixteen and under twenty-one years of age, committed a certain capital offence against father or mother, he was allowed to arrest judgment of death upon himself, by showing that his parents, in the language of the law, 'had been very unchristianly negligent in his education.'"*

And what if the State had been very unchristianly negligent in his education? What if the State have withheld from him, or have suffered to be withheld, during the only course of education provided for him *by* the State, all knowledge of the Word of God, and of the sanctions of religion enforced in that Word?

Speaking again of common schools, and of that religious training necessary for the reason and conscience under a sense of responsibility to God, Mr. Mann remarks: "But if this is ever done, it must be mainly done during the docile and teachable years of childhood. Society is responsible, clergymen are responsible, all are responsible, who can elevate the masses of the people. The conductors of the public press, legislators and rulers, are responsible. In our country and in our times, no man is worthy the honored name of statesman, who does not include the highest practicable education of the people in all his plans of adminis-

* Lectures by Horace Mann, Secretary of the Massachusetts Board of Education.

tration. If this dread responsibility for the fate of our children be disregarded, how can we expect to escape the condemnation, 'Inasmuch as ye have not done it to one of the least of them, ye have not done it unto me.'"

"As educators, as friends and sustainers of the common school system, our great duty is to prepare these living and intelligent souls; to awaken the faculty of thought in all the children of the Commonwealth; to impart to them the greatest practicable amount of useful knowledge; to cultivate in them a sacred regard to truth; to keep them unspotted from the world, that is, uncontaminated from its vices; to train them up to the love of God and the love of man; to make the perfect example of Jesus Christ lovely in their eyes; and to give to all so much religious instruction as is compatible with the rights of others and the gains of our government; and when the children arrive at years of maturity, to commend them to that inviolable prerogative of private judgment and of self-direction, which in a Protestant and Republican country, is the acknowledged birth-right of every human being."

If now we should take at random the various expressions of opinion, from different towns and districts, we should find these sentiments sustained. The conviction is all but universal that a just training of the child in a common school education is impossible in the exclusion of religious instruction. A Report of the School Committee of the city of Salem, Mass., declares that "the sentiment of all parties is that moral instruction and moral consideration ought to have precedence of everything else." In the regulations of the public schools in the town of Swampscot, the following is the fourth section: "The morning exercises of the schools shall commence with the reading of the Bible; and it is recommended that the reading be followed with some devotional service." And so in cases without number, the idea of banishing the Bible and religious instruction as sectarian, would be deemed heathenish.

The Annual Report of the Superintendent of the Public Schools in the city of Boston, remarks, that "the moral feelings, in their early manifestations, appear *first* to the mother's eye, whose light should, like that of the sun falling upon opening flowers, give them the hues of imperishable beauty. But unfortunately for the rising generation, this high parental duty is now so often neglected at home, that many a child must receive at school his first notions of his various duties as a social and an immortal being. True education, in the broad and liberal meaning of the term, includes . . . . such a moulding of the youthful affections and impulses, as will bring them into ready obedience to the voice of conscience, and above all, SUCH RELIGIOUS CULTURE as will aim at imbuing the mind with that Christian spirit which teaches us to love God with all the heart, and our neighbor as ourselves."

This would be impossible, were the Bible and religious instruction excluded from the schools. If the proposed divorce of a common school education from religious truth should be accomplished, where is the "religious culture" that constitutes a primary part of "true education" to be provided or introduced? The affections cannot be rightly moulded, the conscience cannot be trained, without religious instruction.

Mr. Mann applies the same principles to the formation of District Common School libraries, and contends that one grand object of them should be, by the substitution of useful books instead of idle and immoral trash, to protect the children from those temptations and exposures which come from the flood of pernicious reading. "Much can be done by the substitution of books and studies which expound human life and human duty as God has made them to be." "To rear the amaranth of virtue for a celestial soil; to pencil, as with living flame, a rainbow of holy promise and peace upon the blackness and despair of a guilty life; to fit the spirits of weak and erring mortals to shine forever as stars amid the host of heaven; for these diviner and more glorious works, God asks our aid; and He points to children who have been evoked into life as the objects of our labor and care."

"For this purpose, I know of no plan as yet conceived by philanthropy, which promises to be so comprehensive and efficacious as the establishment of good libraries in all our school districts, open respectively to all the children in the State, and within half an hour's walk of any spot upon its surface."

But how is it possible to accomplish this object, if all peculiarly religious truth is first to be expunged from the volumes? How, if at the door of the school district library, a winnowing Index Expurgatorius is to be set up, that shall drive away every religious volume, and blot out from other volumes any pages that may possibly be tinged with a religious bias?

Opinion and Practice in Pennsylvania and New Jersey.

AT the session of the National Convention of the friends of public education, held in Philadelphia in 1850, a Report was presented on the subject of moral and religious instruction in common schools, by the Committee appointed for this purpose.

They remark that "in the common schools, which are, or ought to be, open for the instruction of the children of all denominations, there are many whose religious education is neglected by their parents, and who will grow up in vice and irreligion, unless they receive it from the common school teacher. It seems to us to be the duty of the State to provide for the education of all the children, morally as well as intellectually, and to require all teachers of youth to train the children up in the knowledge and practice of the principles of virtue and piety."

After insisting on the importance, first of all, of teaching by example, they say: "In the next place the Bible should be introduced and read in all the schools in our land. It should be read as a devotional exercise, and be regarded by teachers and scholars as the text-book of morals and religion. The children should early be impressed with the conviction that it was written by inspiration of God, and that their lives should be regulated by its precepts. They should be taught to regard it as the manual of piety, justice, veracity, chastity, temperance, benevolence, and of all excellent virtues. They should look upon this book in connection with the teachings of the Holy Spirit, as the highest tribunal to which we can appeal for the decision of moral questions, and should grow up with the feeling, that the plain declarations of the Bible are the end of all debate. The teacher should refer to this book with reverence. If he have reasons that are clear and satisfactory to his own mind, why he considers the Bible the oracle of divine truth, he may from time to time communicate those reasons to his pupils, if he judges them to be such as they can comprehend.

"We would not recommend the reading of the Scriptures in course, but that the teacher select from day to day the chapter to be read. He may select a portion that commends honesty or veracity, kindness or obedience, the duty of prayer or the keeping of the Sabbath, or the necessity of confessing our faults, or of repenting of our sins. He may tell them why he selects the chapter he does, and may add a few remarks of his own, or mention some incident that will illustrate and enforce the general sentiment. It may be well, when a pupil has violated any moral principle, to read to the school a few verses from the Bible, that they may see how such conduct is regarded by this book."

They add to this the remark: "That it is perfectly easy to communicate moral and religious instruction in the Common Schools without any degree of sectarianism, which is always to be carefully avoided." And they close their precious and admirable report with the following important arguments and suggestions:—

"We believe fully in the necessity of moral and religious instruction, and if the school teacher should neglect it entirely, that very neglect might be an influence on the minds of many children against religion. If the teacher is loved and respected by the children, and gives them no moral instruction, they may conclude that it is because he thinks it unnecessary, and hence they may conclude that it is unnecessary. We recommend the Bible as a sacred volume, to be read as a devotional exercise, or as the text-book of morals and piety. On this basis let him teach all he can, without interfering with the rights of the different denominations of which the school is composed; which we believe opens a larger field in this department of education than most teachers cultivate."

The Board of Directors of the Public Schools of the Fourth Section in Philadelphia recently adopted certain resolutions, in reference to the attempt on the part of the Roman Catholics against the Public School System, among which were the following:

"*Resolved*, That we will ever insist on the reading of the Bible, without note or comment, in our public schools; because, 1st, we believe it to be the Word of God; and, 2d, because we know that such is the will of the vast majority of the commonwealth.

"*Resolved*, That we look on the effort of sectionists to divide the school fund as an insidious attempt to lay the axe t the root of our noble public school system, the benefits of which are every day manifested in the training of the youth.

"*Resolved*, That we will use every means proper for Christians and citizens to employ to maintain our present school system, and to insure the continuance of the reading of God's holy word in all our schools, without respect to consequences, political or otherwise, and we respectfully call on the members of the legislature to respect the rights of the great majority."

Of the opinion on this subject in New Jersey, we may judge something from the following extract from a report by Mr. Halsey, of the Board of Examiners for the County of Middlesex, presented in the Report of the State Superintendent for the year 1850. Speaking of the importance of some work in which "the best modes of imparting moral and religious instruction in the district school, and the importance of such instruction may be thoroughly discussed, and urged upon the mind and heart of the State," he remarks:

"What God has united man may not separate without peril. The children of our schools carry hearts in their bosoms, as well as brains in their heads; now, to separate the head from the heart, to cultivate the one, and neglect the other, is a divorce as unnatural and unchristian as perilous. The child whose hand is educated in elegant and exact penmanship may yet try his acquired art and skill at counterfeiting and forgery, unless his conscience is duly educated. The child whose passions are left untrained aright, whose will is unsubdued, whose lusts are unchecked, when hereafter crossed or roused, may rise upon his parent, take the life of a magistrate, sow sedition on shipboard, fire a court-house or a jail, a dwelling or a prison, or revolutionize his country to effect his fell purpose and reek revenge; revenge for *the robbery of an education without religion, a heart virtually plundered, because deprived of those salutary restraints his fallen nature imperatively needed and God has so bounteously provided.* Nothing, save the fear of God, can be a safeguard against the terrific powers of educated mind, quickened genius, sharpened wit, and enlightened talent, to which it is the aim of our school system to give birth and manhood. How shall this mighty responsibility be safely met, unless parents and teachers be made to feel it, and steadily and earnestly aim at educating the heart and conscience of our children, at home and in the district school? How, unless the Bible be more honored, both as a classic and a class book, and its pages and its truths made familiar to our children? How, unless a higher and holier standard be diligently sought for, in those who have these young hearts, six days out of seven, under their powerful example and tuition?"

Conclusion.

To us, as well as to our fathers, God has spoken: "Therefore shall ye lay up these my words in your heart and in your soul, and bind them for a sign upon your hand, that they may be as frontlets between your eyes. And ye shall teach them to your children, speaking of them when thou sittest in thine house, and when thou walkest by the way, when thou liest down, and when thou risest up. And thou shalt write them upon the door posts of thine house, and upon thy gates." Educated as the Puritans were in the Scriptures, and in the most jealous reverence and love for them, as the foundation both of their civil and ecclesiastical privileges and blessings, they have bequeathed the habit of a religious education, and of the same enshrinement of the Bible in the heart, to all their descendants; a habit, which no attempt was made to undermine, in any part of the country, till the Roman Catholics began the outcry against the Bible and the element of religion in our public schools, as a sectarian thing. But the good ancestral primitive habit is too strong for this infusion of Papal jealousy against the Bible. The decision and firmness of character, which marked our Puritan ancestry, are features of New England still; and New England schools and institutions have got their roots so entwined around the Scriptures, and imbedded in them, that under God's blessing all the miners and sappers of Romanism can do nothing to loosen them.

The same love of the Bible, and sense of our dependence upon it, are increasing elsewhere; and the very attack and insidious effort of Romanism against a common school education with the Bible, as sectarian, tends to awaken the sensitiveness and alarm of the Christian public on a point in regard to which the people had sunk into too sluggish a security. If we would keep our civil freedom, we must educate our children in the Scriptures. That freedom came to us from the Bible ; by the Bible only we can keep it. Like the pillar of cloud by day and of fire by night, Divine Truth led our heroic ancestors through all the sufferings, discipline, and struggles, by which they established our liberties, and nothing else can preserve those liberties, or the spirit of them in their descendants. We must have a religious education ; and if an evil influence should prevail with the State so to change the system to which we have been accustomed as to banish the Bible and religion from it, then the church will be compelled to take it up, as she does the voluntary support of religious worship. In reliance on Christ alone, she has advanced religion more than all State endowments in the world have ever done. In reliance on Christ alone, if compelled into it, she is able to do the same with education. She rejoices in the appropriations of the government for a common school education; but if the condition of such help is to be an oppressive exclusion of the Bible and religious teachings, she abhors the treachery. It would be the death warrant of freedom and religion to put her hand to such a covenant.

There must be an education in religion and morality, or our life as a free people is ended. It is claims from other worlds, according to that noble sonnet of Wordsworth, that have inspirited our star of liberty to rise, and other worlds alone can keep it above the horizon. No earthly expediency, or political management, truckling to the cry of Sectarianism, can save us. Our freedom is the product of celestial wisdom, and not a covenant with the powers of darkness, nor the child of a cunning policy; and celestial wisdom alone can keep it.

> **"What came *from* heaven *to* heaven by nature clings,**
> **And if dissevered thence, its course is short."**

THE END.

www.ingramcontent.com/pod-product-compliance
Lightning Source LLC
LaVergne TN
LVHW020242110826
845151LV00003B/1013